Beyond Slides

Stand out, become irreplaceable, and win big in consulting

Maurizio Cuna

Vatum House

Vatum House

Cover designed by Getcovers
Editing by Pranjal Kumar

First edition: 2025

CONTENTS

To my daughter

Testimonials

Think of Beyond Slides *as Anthony Bourdain's* Kitchen Confidential *but about the opaque industry that is management consulting. Maurizio makes the industry and its characters come alive, packing a punch both in the stories and practical exercises for consultants wanna-bes. You will come away utterly convinced you have the skills and confidence to be a consultant!* – **Tak Lo, Professor, Author of *I, Leader*, and Investor. BearingPoint, Booz Allen Hamilton alumnus**

***

Maurizio has captured timeless insights from his years of on-the-ground experience in Beyond Slides. *This book is an excellent reference for young consultants, who often lack direction and guidance in the fast-paced, high-performance world of consulting. It also serves as a reminder and a reflection for senior executives. What I enjoyed most was the consistent embedding of philosophy, alongside the unmistakable Ancient Roman and Italian flavour you would expect from the author. Highly recommended* – **Anmol Jain, Managing Partner at Infosys Consulting**

***

Maurizio, my mentor and friend from years ahead, has penned a must-read memoir for anyone dreaming of a consulting career or seeking rapid growth at any level. His journey from analyst to partner, rich with global adventures, distills real lessons into candid do's and don'ts and hands-on activities. This book is a universal playbook; Cuna's wisdom shines, offering clear, actionable insights to help every reader navigate and excel in the consulting world – **Mohammed Hassan, Management consultant at PwC**

***

Beyond Slides *by Maurizio Cuna is a standout: a witty, deeply practical guide that reveals the real secrets to thriving in consulting. Cuna, drawing from rich global experience, convincingly argues that true irreplaceability comes from mastering the human element and soft skills, not just polished decks. With actionable exercises and compelling storytelling, this is an indispensable resource for everyone from new joiners to seasoned pros seeking to elevate their game and build a lasting career. A must read* – **Roland Tannous, Entrepreneur and Consultant. Founder of GravityQ, augmenting enterprise performance with GenAI**

***

Consulting is a jungle - fiercely competitive, intellectually demanding, and riddled with ambiguity. The most successful consultants often operate on instinct, having developed a feel for what works - yet rarely pause to explain it, or even know how to. This book cuts through the noise with clarity and precision. It doesn't sugar-coat, theorise endlessly, or leave you guessing. Instead, it offers practical insight into how consulting really works - the unspoken rules, the subtle cues, the strategies that actually make a difference. Whether you're just starting out or already a few years in and looking to level up, this is essential reading – **Marco Mose T., Google Cloud Manager and Tech Entrepreneur. Accenture, EY alumnus**

***

Beyond Slides *distills years of client-side wisdom into clear, actionable lessons. As a former consultant, I was impressed by how quickly the book moves from story to real insights, which is perfect for anyone who wants to hit the ground running in today's corporate world. A concise, practical guide for new consultants that want to create a lasting impact from day one* – **Quilan Foster, McKinsey & Co. alumnus**

***

This book is the practical guide I wish I'd had when I started my consulting journey. It's not just about frameworks and processes - it's about mastering the real skills that drive results: adaptability, building genuine relation-

ships, and embracing serendipity. Each chapter is packed with hard-won lessons and actionable exercises that reflect what I believe truly matters in consulting: integrity, curiosity, and the courage to do things differently. If you want to build a consulting career that lasts and delivers real value for clients, this is your roadmap – **Richard Millington, Consultant and Author, Indispensable Consulting**

***

Beyond Slides *is packed with experiences and stories that lead to actions that you can take to build your career. I found myself laughing at the stories and taking notes to use the strategies that I learned in each chapter. Much of success comes with experience over a long timeframe.* Beyond Slides *shortcuts this by letting you ride along as the author jumps into one situation after another, putting his skills and his BS detector to good use. Highly recommended for anyone in business!* – **Shannon Jean, 10x Founder and Author**

***

Cuna's book peels back the covers of a life as a management consultant that has you nodding profusely, taking notes, and chuckling out loud. Part practical guidebook, part philosophical essay, part autobiography: Cuna explains what's really going on behind the bland job descriptions, fancy office buildings and endless PowerPoint decks. From his writing, you can smell the mood in the boardroom, the tension between team members, the pithy Partner appraisals, and the social decompressing after "pulling an all-nighter." A must-read for anyone who works for/with medium and large consulting organisations, senior leaders at corporations in any country, and for anyone wanting to get tips and tricks on how to influence and grow your career, with humour and integrity. Join Cuna on a professional cultural tour around the world from Puglia to London, Iowa to Hong Kong, and Iceland to Sydney, with plenty of pizza – **Claire Barrett, The Gentle Consultant**

***

What sets this book apart is its brutal honesty and clarity. Unlike the usual consulting career guides that are filled with fluff and buzzwords, this one gets straight to the point. It's written in a style that's refreshingly direct, almost like getting advice from a sharp, experienced colleague over coffee. Having spent years in IT consulting and sales myself, I found it not only accurate but also incredibly insightful. It captures the actual dynamics of our profession: the pressure, the politics, the growth, and the grind. A must-read for anyone who wants a realistic look at what it takes to build a sustainable and rewarding career in consulting – **Franz Petrozzi, Account Executive at SAP. IBM, Infosys alumnus**

***

Reading this book felt like having a conversation with a trusted colleague. The experiences and advice shared are not only incredibly valuable for anyone starting out in consulting, but they also deeply resonated with me. I saw reflections of my own journey in many of the stories, and I appreciated how honestly the author speaks about both the highs and the challenges of this line of work. It's rare to find something that's both so practical and so human - this is exactly the kind of guide I wish I had when I was starting out. I'm sure it will be an eye-opener and a great companion for new joiners **– Zaui Taleb, Banking Consultant. Accenture alumnus**

***

Beyond Slides *is an incredibly insightful look into the world of consulting, how to succeed, avoid pitfalls, and reach your desired outcomes. In the unpredictable world of business, and navigating one's career, having a tested roadmap is invaluable. Throughout my time getting to know Maurizio, I have come to know him as a razor-sharp mind whose insights unlock progress for those lucky enough to know him. This is a must read!* **– John Maher, Founder of Victoriam Group, Financial Services Marketing Consulting**

Foreword

Let me be honest, I'm not a big fan of books and, in particular, I do not like business books. I do not think that most books deserve to exist. I've written a business book and I spent my entire time thinking, *Is this better than someone spending time with their kid or watching a great film, picking a scab, or playing with a puppy?*

I do not like reading them, and I do not like being asked to endorse them, and I do not generally subscribe to the idea that "most people have a book in them." People have egos in them, not ideas that need to exist outside their loving household.

I tried to be miserable about this book, but I kept enjoying it.

Far from five nice blog posts, padded enough to make a book worthy of a spine, this has lots of intel, knowledge, insights even.

I tried to be dismissive about this book, but it offers a unique vantage point into an industry that's needed. That is valuable, that is unusual and helpful, that is unusually free of humblebrags.

What struck me immediately was how unpretentious it is, how readable it is. This is not a book trying to impress you. It is not dressing up basic advice in twenty-dollar words. There is a power to the vulnerability of not hiding behind jargon. Clarity makes our roles seem simple, and that terrifies many. Way too often in the world of consulting we think it's our job to sound like a smart person's idea of a smart person, rather than to form bridges with each other, and to bring people with us.

We're in an interesting time in the world. Technology has entered, smashed into, and created tensions around our world. We as people are not wired to deal with a world that is exponential and global. We are designed for linear and local. We are build for change over generations, for experience to guide us, to have answers to questions we know. We live in the past and the future at the same time; we live dazzled by possibility but frustrated by reality. New experiences - from self-driving cars to 4G download speeds, to VR headsets - move from magical to expected, to how things are, to disappointing in days. The only thing that changes faster than technology is our expectations of it.

There is tension everywhere. Different systems move at different paces. The most vital and valuable layers that underpin the world - etiquette, governance, law, warfare and nuclear power station software - change at a glacial speed, while whimsical companies test and fail their way to hijacking our brain chemistry.

In this relentless but actually rather precedented context, this book is welcome.

It is a smart, punchy, painfully honest look at what it actually takes to survive, and thrive, in consulting, not just in year one, not just until the first promotion, but over the long haul.

The author has been in the trenches. He has travelled, he has eaten bad room service, he has probably worn out more carry-on wheels than most of us own socks. And through all that, he has figured out the quiet stuff, the mindset, the instincts, the habits, that make the difference between burning out fast and building a career that lasts.

There's something rare here: a voice that is honest, sharp, useful, and refreshingly devoid of bullshit. It is personal without being preachy, tactical without being dry. It made me remember why I ever liked this strange world of consulting in the first place, and how easily it eats people alive if they are not careful.

If you are just getting started in consulting, or you have made it in but can already feel the cracks forming, *Beyond Slides* is the book you should read before you start quoting "strategy" in your sleep.

It will not tell you how to win at PowerPoint. It will not teach you how to "crack a case." Instead, it will give you a roadmap for staying sharp, growing deliberately, and avoiding the corporate slow death of becoming really good at things that do not matter.

You might even enjoy reading it.

I did. And that, my friend, is truly rare.

—

Tom Goodwin

Founder of business consulting firm *All We Have Is Now*

Bestselling author of *Digital Darwinism: Survival of the Fittest in the Age of Business Disruption*

A NOTE FROM THE AUTHOR

There are two ways to learn in life.

The first is by trial and error, the way our ancestors figured out which mushrooms were poisonous, by watching someone else die from eating them. The second is by absorbing the wisdom of those who have already made the mistakes for you, which is far less lethal but, for some reason, much less popular.

This book is my attempt to save you a few unnecessary bruises.

If you are curious about consulting but have no idea what it actually entails beyond LinkedIn posts filled with words like "impact" and "value", this book is for you.

If you are already in the business world and find yourself questioning whether you took the right path or just need an edge to accelerate, this book is for you.

And if you are fresh into the consulting world, trying to navigate the political minefield and figure out why your slides keep coming back with 37 comments, then, yes, this book is especially for you.

I have had mentors who changed my career trajectory: a manager who put me up for my first promotion, a leader who pushed me toward partnership earlier than I thought possible. These were people who saw in me something I did not yet see in myself.

Yes, mentors help. But they do not do the work for you.

It was still on me to leave my homeland, Italy, at 23, work ridiculous hours, and solve problems that often had no clear solutions. I had to take risks, stumble through the learning curves, and, importantly, know when to shut up and listen. While my mentors were invaluable, they could only teach me so much. Some lessons, you have to trip over yourself.

This book is about those lessons.

Right now, I feel as good as I have ever felt professionally. I know what I am good at, what I am terrible at, and, critically, what does not matter. For the most part, I am proud of what I have achieved so far, but at a certain point in your career, you realize that success is no longer about what you can do, but what you can build.

At the higher levels, this game is about leadership, not in the LinkedIn-inspirational-quote sense, but in the *who can I trust to handle things so I do not have to?* sense. The best leaders are the ones who nurture the next crop, who recognize that their real value is in building people, not in micromanaging them.

This book is about the little things I wish I had known when I started: the real knowledge (not the stuff you pick up from corporate training modules), the things you only grasp after you have made the mistakes. If I hand some of those ideas to you in advance, you will get where you want to be faster and with fewer battle scars.

The consulting world overemphasizes hard skills: data visualization, process mapping, Excel wizardry, coding. Sure, these are useful, but they are table stakes. Nobody ever got promoted to Partner because they were great at VLOOKUP. Real success comes from everything else: how you think, communicate, and navigate power structures. Ignore this, and you are voluntarily putting a cap on your career before it even begins.

These days, it is trendy to dunk on consulting. People call it extractive, soul-crushing, a pyramid scheme in a suit. And look, I am not here to defend the late-night decks or the overuse of frameworks that explain nothing, but let us zoom out. Every powerful civilization had a *consulting* class: advisors, scribes, senates, viziers, mandarins. People who sat close to decision-makers, not because they had the final say, but because they could synthesize complexity and articulate what actually mattered.

Modern consulting, whatever its flaws, is the continuation of that tradition. It is now no longer just about giving advice; increasingly, consulting is about execution. You do not simply tell the client what to do, but you often have to build it, test it, land it, and make it stick. That means consultants are no longer just thinkers, but are builders, translators, problem-and-solution-whisperers who live at the intersection of strategy and operations. If you pay attention, this hybrid role teaches you how to navigate ambiguity and deliver results.

These are skills that make you lethal in any field you touch after.

The truth is, most people who sneer at consulting were never good at it: they bounced off the surface and blamed the surface. For those who understand the game, and use it as a launchpad, not a cage, it is still one of the most asymmetric bets in the professional world.

This book is for those who want to make that bet wisely.

I have a lot of faith in the next generation. Contrary to the complaints of bitter old men, they are more ambitious, driven, and, in many cases, more competent than my peers and I were at their age. My goal is to accelerate their learning curve.

In October of 2023, I lost my father to cancer. Two months before he left our world, he finally published his book of poetry and short fiction, pieces he had been writing and sharing with friends on loose sheets for decades. His author bio says it was his first published work, but I know the truth: that book was thirty years late. For as long as I can remember, there were always handwritten notebooks scattered around the house, scribbled in pencil or typed out on an old machine. As I grew up, he would pick the project back up every few years with new energy, convinced this time he would finish it.

But life got in the way, or maybe fear did, and he only got around to doing it when time had already run out.

I realized I did not want to leave sharing my opinions and passions until my deathbed. Of course, this book is not filled with meaningful Italian verses, but it is my way of passing something forward: a blueprint, a shortcut, a set of signposts for those coming up behind me.

This book will have done its job if it saves you even a few wasted years.

Reading Map

Beyond Slides opens with a Prequel, my version of a *book trailer*, told in words rather than moving images, followed by an Introduction. The main body consists of 13 chapters (and a bonus one) packed with insights to build a sustainable and high-impact career in the consulting and corporate world.

In the first four chapters we will talk about how to make serendipity your friend (Chapter 1), a new way of thinking about networking (Chapter 2), how to speak the lingo so you walk into any room sounding like you belong (Chapter 3), and how to turn feedback into fertilizer (Chapter 4).

After that, we are going to discuss what we can learn from anti-mentors (Chapter 5), how to bend the rules in your favor (Chapter 6), some actionable ideas on taking ownership of your time (Chapter 7), and the ways to become a global consultant (Chapter 8).

Finally, I will share some ideas around becoming an intrapreneurial consultant that thinks like a start-up CEO (Chapter 9), we will find out why humor is your Trojan horse (Chapter 10), how to turn reputation into a hard currency (Chapter 11), the ways to unearth your intrinsic engine no bonus can match (Chapter 12), and, in closing, why you should never take a shortcut in this business (Chapter 13).

Every story you are about to read is honest, straight from the trenches of my own experience: these are backroom lessons. Yes, I have changed a few names and details, partly to avoid some awkward encounters at industry conferences, partly because it's fun to keep people guessing, and mainly because the truth works best when mixed with a bit of fiction.

Let me be clear: this is not a hit piece. The characters in these cautionary tales are often a patchwork of real people, a Frankenstein of mediocrity, hubris, brilliance, and occasional flashes of genius. I am not here to settle scores or indulge in some petty *exposé*. If you recognize yourself on these pages, that's good. Don't take it personally; in fact, take it as an opportunity. If you do not recognize yourself... well, you might want to double-check that your head is not stuck in the clouds of self-delusion.

To make things easier to digest, each chapter includes a closing *vignette*: a textual cinematic strip featuring two characters I hope you soon will grow fond of. Ivy is the eager, thoughtful, and curious student trying to navigate the labyrinth of consulting. Morrie is the wise mentor who has seen enough nonsense to fill a few Wikipedia pages. Their conversations are designed to make you reflect, chuckle, and most importantly, absorb the lessons in a way that feels real rather than scripted.

Because knowledge without action is as useless as an espresso machine with no coffee beans, each chapter closes with three practical exercises. These are not some HR-approved *reflection prompts* designed to make you feel good about doing nothing (for the HR professionals reading, I'm kidding!). These are deliberate practice drills meant to take what you have read and force it into your muscle memory. There are 39 in total. That sounds like a lot, but it is not meant to overwhelm you.

Think of them as a one-year boot camp for your consulting brain: targeted and simple, but also powerful when repeated over time. Remember that you are learning a craft here, not cramming for an exam. These exercises are designed to be sharp moves that you can revisit, refine, and slowly internalize – not all at once, but slowly, then suddenly.

They will form your *Consultant's Journal*, a living record of your growth, insights, and occasionally bruised ego. Take it seriously, and you will not just read about becoming a great consultant; you will become one.

Finally, in the Appendix, you will find a summary of the key insights from each chapter, distilled into simple and easy-to-scan bullet points. Use the section to refresh your memory whenever you need to pick up the thread or spark a fresh insight down the line.

Whether you are at the start of your consulting journey or already a few years in, this book could be your blueprint for building an inspired career. Like any blueprint, it's only as valuable as the effort you put into executing it.

Shall we begin?

Allow me to show you what *actually* consulting looks like beyond slides.

Sydney, 15th June 2025

Maurizio Cuna

PREQUEL

I slam the alarm clock shut as the red neon numbers flash 5:30 am. My palms cup my face. Eyes open. A quick reminder: work starts in an hour. I get up. Splash some cold water on my face. The mind catches up with the body. Through the massive windows of my suite at the Grand Hyatt in Hong Kong, I spot a group of old men performing *tai chi* in the park. Slow, deliberate movements, like a synchronized conspiracy against arthritis.

The city hums in the background, a mix of car horns, ferry horns, and the occasional distant shout. A cool breeze sneaks in through the gap in the sliding door. My girlfriend sleeps on the other side of the bed, knowing full well that by the time she wakes up, I will be gone, whisked away to the client's office, another twelve-hour day ahead.

When I first met Kristie in London, she asked me what I did for work.

"I am a management consultant," I said.

She squinted. "So what do consultants do?"

The dreaded question: the consulting Rorschach test.

My usual response: "I solve business problems for people".

"For companies, you mean?"

"Companies are made of people," I countered. "Their services affect people. I am basically a therapist for businesses."

She did not even flinch. "Ah. So you are kind of a prostitute?"

Now, I could have defended myself with an elaborate justification. I could have explained that implementation work requires skin in the game and that risk-averse organizations need external parties to identify the blind spots their people are too entangled to see.

But she used to work in a bank and, frankly, her analogy was much funnier than mine.

"We all charge by the hour and aim to extend our services," I admitted.

Before I shower, I step onto the balcony. Ritual. A daily pause before the chaos begins. Staring at the horizon just before sunrise is the closest you can get to feeling like the last human alive, especially in a city like Hong Kong, where history, power, and absurd amounts of money swirl together like an expensive cocktail from a random rooftop in Lan Kwai Fong.

I am 9,000 kilometers from my birthplace, a sleepy southern Italian town that would have laughed at the idea of me living this life. I have dragged myself across the world for clients, chasing a future that once seemed unfathomable.

The sky transitions from deep, brooding blue to slashes of yellow and orange. This is my cue. It's time to move.

Dressed. Egg mayo sandwich in hand, yesterday's room service, because I am both practical and slightly self-destructive. I step into the elevator.

Ding. Doors open.

Inside, my companion for the descent is a Lady of the Night.

She wears a shiny miniskirt, an impractical choice at 6:15 am unless, of course, you have been working the night shift.

The elevator hums. Silence. I chew my sandwich. She checks her phone.

And yet, despite *the views*, all I can think about is the mess waiting for me at the client's office. This engagement is in shambles, and I am once again giving myself the pep talk that keeps me going:

> *Management consulting is brutal. But nothing is more rewarding than when you pull off a great project and a client shakes your hand. Few careers are this varied and stimulating. You work with brilliant, knowledgeable, and often influential people worldwide. It is more of a lifestyle than a job, really. I cannot imagine doing anything else.*

The elevator dings again. The doors slide open, and my ride awaits: a dented red Toyota Crown Comfort with a driver who looks like he has been chain-smoking since the British handover. He exhales a plume of smoke, flicks his cigarette out the window with the precision of a man who has done it a thousand times, and nods at me like we are old war buddies. No words exchanged, other than my destination address delivered in my best local language: *Sītúbá Dào*. An unspoken agreement: *You get in, I get you there, and we both pretend mornings are not real.*

The Lady? She heads to the basement and exits through the back door: her agreement with the hotel is that she never walks through the lobby.

She probably has a better ride waiting for her than I had.

Introduction

You have landed your dream consulting gig. You bought a business suit, your first real one, not the awkward rental you wore to graduation, or the Zara blazer that never quite sat right. For the guys, it might be a sharp navy number with just enough shoulder structure to say *I mean business*. For the women, maybe a tailored dress you tried on seventeen times, debating whether it was *powerful* or just *trying too hard*. The shoes are black, stiff, and slightly uncomfortable. Whether they have heels or not, they feel like an idea of adulthood you are still getting used to. But they look the part.

You are stepping into the management consulting labyrinth, wide-eyed and slightly overwhelmed, but armed with a dangerous confidence level. You probably know your way around Excel better than your neighborhood. You format cells with the precision of a Renaissance artist and throw together sleek PowerPoint slides with an aesthetic that could make Sandro Botticelli jealous. You think these things matter.

They may do, for now.

I get it. I was exactly where you are. I know that none of it will play out the way you think. Let me tell you a small, inconvenient secret that most consultants learn too late after years of mistaking *busyness* for *effectiveness*: your ego is your most significant liability. Are you ready to kill it?

Mastering SQL, financial modeling, and the endless parade of Excel gymnastics is easy. Step-by-step, module by module, tutorial by tutorial: anyone with a Wi-Fi connection and mild caffeine addiction can do it. But there is no Coursera course for making clients remember your name ten years from now. No certification in being the kind of consultant they call first when things go sideways. The question I wish someone had slapped me with, preferably over a strong Italian espresso at a dingy café, is this: "Are you ready to pour an ungodly amount of time into sharpening your soft skills?" Not *working on them*, not *being aware of them*, but sharpening them, like a blade, every damn day.

You can be the best number cruncher in the room, but if you cannot read the politics swirling around a boardroom, if you cannot sense when a client is bullshitting you, or if you cannot disarm an executive with a well-timed joke, you will hit a ceiling so hard it will leave a dent.

Consulting is a people business. No, really. Not the fake "people business" nonsense you often read on corporate mission statements; consulting *actually* runs on human psychology, egos, and trust. You might think you are an analytical assassin, slicing through inefficiencies with your spreadsheet katana. However, at some point, you will find yourself in a room with an executive who is paying you $500 per hour to validate what his gut has already told him.

Welcome to the actual job.

The naïve consultant believes that consulting is about intelligence, about finding *the* answer. Instead, the game is rigged: the answer is often already known. Your job is not to discover fire but to make the fire palatable to people who are afraid of getting burned. This is where soft skills come in. Most consultants, especially the young ones, treat soft skills as an HR-induced fever dream and believe raw intelligence and SQL querying skills will carry them. The result is that they talk too much in meetings, obsess over their own slides, and fundamentally misunderstand that business problems are 90% human.

Sustaining a long-term successful career in consulting is like playing chess, where the chessboard is rotating, a few pawns are missing, the queen has a beef with the bishop, and your senior client just replaced the knight with a horse from his ranch because he *likes that horse better*. Strategy is essential, but psychology wins the game.

The ability to look at client executives and understand whether they want a *solution* or just *someone to blame*, reading a client's silence better than another consultant's report, adapting in real time when the strategy you spent three months perfecting gets obliterated in a single board meeting, quickly understanding how to rescue a project where the shit hit the fan (it always happens): these are some of the things that separate the good consultants from the *great* ones.

The best consultants do not just solve problems: they make themselves irresistible. If you are merely a problem-solver, you are replaceable. If you are the one people trust to solve problems, you are untouchable. So yes, keep refining your deck and memorizing your industry frameworks; however, know that you are not a consultant if you cannot handle human complexity and navigate fragile egos and misaligned incentives. At best, you are a glorified PowerPoint operator that soon nobody will remember.

My first office was so small that I am convinced somebody previously used it to store janitorial supplies. It had the ambiance of a neglected basement, the air quality of a Turkish bathhouse, and a coffee machine that produced something vaguely resembling burnt motor oil. None of that mattered: I was a young consultant, armed with perfect spreadsheets, ready to impress my client. Except, the client did not give a damn about my numbers. He skimmed through them like they were yesterday's lottery results and moved on. That was my first real lesson in consulting: technical brilliance means *jack shit* if you cannot connect with people.

Fast-forward 20 years, and I am still navigating the same labyrinth, except now the numbers (and the egos I deal with) are more considerable. I have run multi-million-dollar programs with teams spread across continents, consulted for Fortune 500s, and, most importantly, learned to avoid assuming people make decisions based on logic. Do not get me wrong: I am not unique in any way. I am no genius or prodigy. I am a competitive sponge, soaking up knowledge faster than most while being slightly more stubborn about improvement. That alone has been enough.

I grew up in a small village in southern Italy, just outside the city of Lecce in an area named *Salento*, where olive trees outnumber children and the Mediterranean Sea feels like it is breathing right outside your door. I had no blue-chip connections and absolutely zero exposure to the world of high finance or strategy, but I did have a rigorous education: Italian literature, Latin, Ancient Greek, Philosophy (the classics). I finished school two years ahead of my peers, mostly because I *could*, I *wanted to,* and, well, the administrators let me. "Exceptional school merits," they called it (who knows if they were right).

Then came university: Padua, the same place where Galileo Galilei used to teach (that is where any comparisons to geniuses *immediately* end). I studied Computer Science because, at the time, computers were *the* thing. I had no idea what Silicon Valley was up to, but I was obsessed with understanding technology and its potential. Then, something unexpected happened: consulting snuck up on me.

It started with Paolo, an older friend who had just landed a job at Accenture. He was not one for fake enthusiasm, so when he had *zero* complaints about consulting, I figured it must be at least tolerable. Over pizza, he told me about the projects, the travel, the excitement. That was enough for me to think, *Well, I guess I can quit drumming in my punk-rock band for this.* A few months later, Accenture came recruiting at my university. They seemed reasonable, they offered me a decent salary, so *why not?* My bandmates are still pissed off with me for selling out to corporate life, but to be fair, they still play in the same bars for free beer.

Consulting chose me more than I chose it. I had *no* clue what I was getting into. Within a year, I pulled off a minor miracle: landing a consulting job in the UK without knowing a single word of English (Pro tip: Enthusiasm can occasionally replace competence, at least in the short term.) That kicked off two decades of working across nine countries, four continents, and countless cultural landmines. Somehow, I survived, not because I am brilliant, but because I had the good sense to stick with great mentors and absorb their wisdom like my life depended on it. Consulting is a game of endurance and adaptation (plus, as I always say, knowing when to shut up), and if you master *that*, you can go from broom closet to boardroom faster than you think.

These days, the corporate world is drowning in books, guides, and think-pieces written by people who have either (a) never worked in an actual corporation or (b) are lifers who somehow missed the plot despite decades on the inside. Consulting books are no different: most are half-assed PowerPoint decks stretched into 200 pages. This is *not* one of those books.

This book is also *not* a few other things.

This book is *not* the gospel. It is *not* the ultimate, earth-shattering guide to consulting. It is *not* a manifesto with "10X secrets" or moonshot dreams. What is it, then? I believe it is something rare: a collection of answers to the questions young consultants *actually* ask.

You can spend hours scavenging the internet, listening to long all-noise-no-signal podcasts, watching recycled TED Talks, filtering through YouTube gurus whose biggest project is managing their own delusions of grandeur, *or* you can spend the next 3 hours here and save yourself years of learning the hard way.

Your call.

I am not in the habit of agreeing with the French, but philosopher André Gide (annoyingly) had a point when he said: "Everything that needs to be said has already been said. But since no one was listening, everything must be said again."

It is the curse of wisdom: truth rarely arrives with fireworks. It whispers but people prefer noise. They mistake novelty for insight and style for substance. They forget that repetition is reinforcement.

So yes, we must say it all again. And again. Like monks with a drum. Like your grandmother reminding you not to marry an idiot.

Because the problem is not that people do not *know*. The problem is that knowing does not stick, and so the old truths, even if boring, painful and perhaps unfashionable, must be reframed.

We forget. And the price of forgetting is always paid in sweat or regret.

This book will not teach you how to perfectly polish your shoes or which tie will supposedly impress a client (hint: nobody cares). It will, however, help you decode corporate landmines in the modern environment: how to handle a passive-aggressive client without losing your sanity, how to navigate office politics when you are *not* the one holding the power, how to keep your career intact while missing weddings, birthdays, and family dinners because some exec needs a "quick update" at 10 pm. Some of you will call these insights "hacks." I hate that term. Hacks imply shortcuts, a cheap trick to bypass real work. Consulting is *work*, and real professionals do not cut corners. But if by "hack" you mean optimizing your approach, rethinking norms, and breaking problems wide open, then fine, I will accept it. Because that is what consulting *should* be.

In essence, this is not a cheat sheet but a playbook for strategic maneuvering through the political, psychological and logistical minefield that is management consulting. You can think of me as the cool uncle at a barbecue, handing out wisdom between sips of red wine (preferably, an *Amarone della Valpolicella*), or the espresso-drinking *signore* who wants you to succeed without making the same dumb mistakes I did.

Charles Darwin said it best: "It is not the strongest or the smartest who survive, but the ones who adapt."

That is what this book is about: helping you *adapt* and *thrive* in the modern corporate jungle. Because make no mistake: it *is* a jungle, and only the sharp survive.

Serendipity Strikes Those Who Seek It

14th-century philosopher Jean Buridan met his end in a way that would make even the most hardened intellectuals chuckle, if not shift uncomfortably in their chairs. The man, a celebrated logician, was allegedly stuffed into a sack and tossed into the Seine by an angry mob. Some say it was because he seduced the wrong woman (classic), the Queen of France specifically, others because his students had grown tired of his intellectual games. Whatever the reason, one can only imagine the final moments: a mind that had spent decades dissecting the nature of free will, now trapped in a sack, bobbing in the filthy Parisian water, trying to out-argue the laws of physics.

Buridan's most famous contribution to philosophy is a thought experiment about an *ass* (that is, a donkey, not the anatomical region) so rational that it starves to death, unable to choose between a stack of hay and a pail of water placed precisely at the same distance. Jean Buridan, on the other hand, was not given the luxury of hesitation. His students did not suffer from *analysis paralysis*; they picked the river, and that was it. Ironically, had the donkey behaved a little less like an ass (pun intended), had it just stumbled left or right out of sheer impulse, it would have lived.

And therein lies a hidden lesson: serendipity thrives on movement. When you are stuck, when options seem equally good (or bad), waiting for the perfect answer is a slow death. Pick something. Anything. Trip over your own feet if you must. The best outcomes in life often come from the simple yet uncomfortable act of not standing still.

When you are just beginning your consulting career, the unpredictability and pace of everyday life can feel both exhilarating and overwhelming. It is pure chaos, but chaos is not inherently destructive. Serendipity is the shy cousin that chaos feels obligated to bring to the party. Serendipity can be magic; if one embraces it, serendipity can be used as an active tool for career development.

First off, let's debunk the notion that serendipity is luck. It's not. It's what Nassim Taleb calls "positive exposure to randomness." You position yourself in the line of potential opportunity to be ready when it's time to strike and exploit the chance that just happens to fall in your lap. It's more than just being at the right place at the right time; it's about placing yourself strategically at multiple *right places* as often as possible.

This is the first idea we discuss in the book because I genuinely owe my entire career to serendipity: nothing in my younger years suggested I would end up advising leaders across the world. I had a degree in *Computer Science*, which meant I was supposed to build things. Instead, I found myself at Accenture in Milan, Italy, where the main thing I was building was my tolerance for Word documents and late nights. Consulting 101. The first few months were a blur of jargon, Excel sheets, PowerPoint slides, and pretending to know what I was doing. Still, about a year in, after enough mind-numbing tasks to make a lesser man reconsider his life choices, I had an epiphany: I liked the job.

Do not get me wrong. I did not enjoy working till midnight because some overambitious manager had promised a client the moon on a deadline that could barely deliver a pebble. I did not enjoy dragging myself home, exhausted and starving, only to find the local *Pizzeria Partenopea* closed and be forced into a tragic, stomach-growling sleep. But I was learning. Learning how to work. Learning how to talk to clients. Learning, importantly, that competence is a form of power. The problem was not the *What.* It was the *Where.* I wanted out, out of Italy, specifically. I was 23, had never left the country, and spoke English at a level best described as "tourist lost in London who never visited London before". My vocabulary included "Hello", "My name is", and sheer optimism.

Most people would have stopped there. Most people did indeed whisper to me: "You do not speak English. How do you expect to land a job abroad?"

I had a different thought process: I would apply anyway. The worst-case scenario is a bunch of rejection emails, and rejection emails are just digital waste. Noise. Background radiation. All I needed was one *yes*, and my life would change.

Luckily, my roommate, Giosue, was equally restless. When I pitched my master plan (blindly applying to random jobs on LinkedIn), he nodded and said, "Why not?", and that was the full extent of our strategy session. This was in the early days of LinkedIn, back when it was still a *tool*, not a theater, before it got hijacked by corporate monks writing self-congratulatory sermons and fake vulnerability posts ending with "and that's when I learned the power of kindness." I know it sounds incredible now, but at that time LinkedIn was all about job listings, recruiters who replied, and a search bar that actually led somewhere!

At first, I aimed for the U.S., until I realized visas were a bureaucratic nightmare. The UK, still in the European Union then, seemed more manageable. So we went all-in. For a month, we carpet-bombed every job posting that vaguely resembled entry-level consulting, armed with tailored CVs, carefully worded cover letters, and a blind faith in probability. Then, miracle of miracles, I started getting phone interviews. Minor problem: I barely spoke English. These calls were a tragicomic loop of "Sorry?" "Can you repeat that?" and long, panicked silences. I understood nothing, but I kept going. I started watching movies in English, classics like *Top Gun*, *Mission: Impossible*, and *Rocky* (intellectual choices, I know, but they helped!).

And one day, serendipity hit.

How to get a job sitting in a Starbucks

I got a call from an Icelandic firm trying to set up shop in London: a tiny outfit, barely on the map, looking for an enthusiastic junior consultant (which, in corporate-speak, translates to cheap, desperate, and willing to endure mild exploitation). Perfect. That was me. I was already working like a dog, so if I was going to burn through my youth chasing some ill-defined corporate hotshot dream, I might as well do it somewhere exciting, somewhere that did not remind me of my high school commute.

Then came a revelation: speaking English with someone who was not a native speaker was like suddenly unlocking a cheat code. The Managing Director from Reykjavík spoke slowly, clearly, like a man who understood the existential horror of language barriers. I grasped 70% of what he said, a quantum leap from the 10% I managed when speaking with native English interviewers. The guy liked us. He invited both my friend Giosue and me for an in-person interview.

In London.

On Sunday.

He was flying in from Madrid, fresh off picking up his MBA diploma, because apparently, real corporate warriors collect those like Pokémon badges. He suggested we meet at a Starbucks near Heathrow, *en route* from the airport.

We were ecstatic. We packed our best suits and flew to London. (Side note: this was my first time on a plane. No pressure.) Fresh out of our budget hostel in Earl's Court that Sunday morning, we strutted into Starbucks looking absurdly elegant. I have never dressed that formally since, not even for my own wedding!

The MD arrived, and he took us in one by one. I went first.

At the table, he grabbed a napkin and began sketching the bank's technology landscape, the one I would soon be working with. It was complex, intricate, and miles ahead of anything I had seen in my brief consulting career. I nodded like a seasoned expert, pitched a couple of ideas, tossed in some naïvely enthusiastic opinions, but, mostly, I played to my strengths:

1) I was young

2) I was eager

3) I was not an idiot

I made it clear: "Tell me what to learn, and I will learn it." My foundation was solid: an excellent education, decent experience at a big-name consulting firm, and an unshakable willingness to grind. It worked.

A few days after returning to Italy, we both got job offers. London, here we come.

There was only one small formality left: the dreaded reference check.

Typically, this would not be a big deal, but there was a tiny issue: I did not want my current boss to know I was looking for another job. If she found out, my life at Accenture would turn into a corporate gulag, and the last thing I needed was a guilt-tripping, passive-aggressive manager breathing down my neck for betraying the sacred bond of consulting servitude.

So, I had to get creative.

Luckily, my friend Monte also worked at Accenture. Monte was one of those guys who could talk his way into (or out of) anything, the kind of guy who could show up to a Michelin-starred restaurant in flip-flops and somehow convince the maître d' that he was a visiting food critic. He had the natural charisma of a seasoned diplomat combined with the mischief of a high schooler trying to convince his teacher that his dog ate his homework.

When I explained the situation, he immediately saw the humor in it.

"So let me get this straight," he said. "You want me to pretend to be your manager and give you a glowing reference?"

Exactly.

A few days later, the Icelandic firm HR called him for the reference check. I waited anxiously for an update, half expecting him to crack under pressure and start improvising nonsense. When he called me afterward, I could hear the barely contained laughter in his voice: "Mate, you owe me a drink. I think I just convinced them you are the second coming of James Oscar McKinsey himself. The guy sounded so impressed that he was probably taking notes for his own career. You are in."

And that was it. The reference check was a roaring success, and the job was officially mine. Looking back, that whole episode still makes me smile. Monte was more than a friend; he would do anything for his people and never ask *why*, just *how far?* Sadly, he is gone now, taken far too young by cancer in his early thirties.

Losing him was a gut punch, but every time I think about this story, I can still hear his voice and see his smirk as he bragged about how he had sold me as the future of consulting.

That is how I secured my first international job: with a bit of serendipity, some audacity, and one of the best references in consulting history.

I moved to the UK and, to be fair, the money was not great, but what could I expect?! The small Icelandic venture in London was hiring two kids with a year of work experience who didn't know enough English to order a sandwich (true story, I'll tell you all about it a little later).

I had banked solely on Lady Luck and ended up securing a job in England without speaking fluent English. There were countless logical and practical reasons why it should not have worked out, but I gambled on a bit of chance, and it paid off.

Think about that.

Serendipity in your early years of consulting

Early in your consulting career, you will likely work on a broad spectrum of projects.

A year into the job, you might be crafting a market entry strategy for a tech start-up and then switching to analyzing procurement efficiencies for a manufacturing giant. During this stage, it is understandable if you think, "How am I ever going to specialize?" However, the revolving door of projects is anything but random. These are *career door openers*.

You are dabbling in different sectors and roles without any long-term commitment. But you are not being thrown around aimlessly; you are collecting a portfolio of *bets*, each with its own risk and reward profile. The more randomness you allow into your career, the more resilient you become; strength is built through exposure to volatility, not by hiding from it. Every high-risk project you tackle, every new problem you solve, feeds into your ability to handle the unknown, and you start to learn how to benefit from ambiguity.

Think of it like venture capitalism... but for your career: you are spreading out your investments so that one successful exit (or, in your case, a killer project) can offset the other not-so-great ventures.

You need to play these bets smartly, similar to what I did when applying for jobs in England, allowing for a few rejection letters here and there.

When given the chance, gravitate toward work where the risks are clear but the rewards are hard to cap.

Choice is one of the most underrated privileges in the corporate world. A lack of agency over one's work, especially when it becomes routine, is a major source of dissatisfaction, but that does not mean options do not exist. They do. The catch is they rarely land in your lap.

You have to be strategic, persistent, and a little stubborn to spot and earn them.

Of course, early on, it does not feel like that. At the start of your career, you barely choose which project you are staffed on, let alone where the client is located. You do not get a say in the coffee machine: sometimes, *you are the coffee machine.*

The absence of choice today does not mean permanent powerlessness. What feels like servitude now is often just your first exposure to the system you will later learn to bend. Get familiar with this line of thinking if you want to be in this business for the long haul.

During your early years, as you understand the organization's workings and acclimatize to the world of consulting, spend time building trust and a friendly relationship with your leaders and your schedulers (the people who will send you off to projects). All professional services are just a pursuit of understanding what people want and offering them ways to achieve that.

If the decision makers notice you, trust you, and like having you around, you do not sit in the basket waiting to be picked, unlike the others. You stroll the orchard and choose the tree. Everyone else is just ripening for someone else's harvest.

Let's say you finally achieved that degree of optionality, and now you have the opportunity to choose between a well-defined market research gig for a Fortune 500 company or a slightly nebulous project for a promising healthcare start-up.

As a consultant, the former has a limited upside: it will look good on your resume but won't be a game-changer.

The latter is a wild card. If it succeeds, you are part of the team of prodigies who foresaw the future of healthcare. If it fails, you still gain a unique experience that sets you apart from the rest of consulting spreadsheet warriors.

When possible, always go for the gigs that could make you a legend: these are your asymmetric bets, with low downside and disproportionate reward.

For example, after a few years of working in London, I was offered the opportunity to move to Hong Kong to work on a high-profile, struggling project on the verge of failing.

That engagement involved a technology I had never dealt with, in a continent I had never visited before, and for an industry I knew nothing about. Naturally, I said *Yes!* If I pulled it off, the career boost would be enormous. If I failed, I would at least have a hell of a story to tell over drinks. We delivered, and I ended up scoring two promotions from that one project.

As you are placing your career bets, embrace what I call *calculated randomness*. Attend that random networking event where everyone looks like they were manufactured in the same corporate factory. Read up on technologies you barely understand, not because you plan to master them but because you might just trip over a golden insight while fumbling in the dark. Talk to people you would usually never speak to: the wild-eyed AI researcher, the aging marketing guru, the eccentric entrepreneur with shoes so shiny you can see your disappointed reflection in them. Innovation is a bit like hunting for truffles, and you are the pig snuffling around for the good stuff when he does not know where the good stuff exactly hides.

Surprises teach us that the world is surprising

In 1928, Alexander Fleming was just going about his usual routine at St. Mary's Hospital in London when, one day, he accidentally left a petri dish of *Staphylococcus bacteria* uncovered near an open window. Classic hygiene fail: it got contaminated with mold while he was off on holiday (because, of course). When he came back, he could have tossed the dish straight into the bin, but instead, he took a closer look and realized the bacteria surrounding the mold were dead. Dead! What he had stumbled upon was *Penicillium notatum*, the first-ever antibiotic, penicillin, the thing that has probably saved more lives than clean water and seat belts combined. It all happened because he was willing to pause and say, "What the hell is this?" instead of "Damn, I fucked up."

Fleming was not trying to discover antibiotics; he just kept his eyes open for weirdness and acted on it. That is the essence of calculated randomness: the more of it you allow into your career, the more chances you have to trip over something spectacular. And when you do, you better be ready to pounce on it like your future depends on it, because it just might. When you diversify your knowledge and network, you increase the surface area for serendipity to strike.

Daniel Kahneman, Nobel laureate and the godfather of behavioral economics, once said, "The correct lesson to learn from surprises is that the world is surprising," and yes, this is the same guy who spent his entire life exposing how flawed and deluded the human mind can be at predicting anything. You can map out your career with the precision of Renzo Piano designing *The Shard* (minus the ugliness), but life will still turn around, laugh at your meticulous little blueprint, and set it on fire. The Titanic's route looked magnificent on paper until a chunk of floating ice appeared. Mike Tyson nailed it when he said, "Everybody has a plan till they get punched in the face." The punch is coming.

Central planning did not work for Stalin; it won't work for you either. The man tried to engineer an entire society down to the last potato and ended up with a lot of starvation, misery, and gulags. Are you trying to plan your whole career to precision? Good luck. Your life is not a strategy deck, but a rolling mess where the best opportunities are off-script and unscheduled because the universe does not care about your little Gantt chart. Instead of trying to bulldoze the future into submission, learn to dance with randomness.

I hope I have convinced you by now that randomness, when embraced, becomes optionality. And optionality is power: it's the ability to seize opportunities you never planned for but are smart enough to recognize. This is where serendipity creates the conditions for randomness to reward you.

Open yourself up to the world's chaos. Court randomness like a lover who always leaves you wanting more. Set traps for serendipity and be ready to spring into action when the universe throws you a bone. Take it as a lifestyle, a conscious constant calculating risks and rewards.

In the next chapter, I will show you how to turn networking (yes, the dreaded word) into your best tool for engineering serendipity and finding career-defining opportunities.

***

Vignette

Office kitchenette in the morning. Whir of an overworked coffee machine. Ivy dabs at a smoothie stain on her shirt. Morrie, oddly serene, watches his toast in the toaster like it owes him money.

Ivy: So, I told my manager I wanted to be staffed on a "strategic transformation," and she goes, "Perfect. There's this urgent reporting clean-up in Supply Chain."
Morrie: Classic. Strategy adjacent.
Ivy: I spent three weeks color-coding Excel rows like I was prepping them for kindergarten.
Morrie: That is strategy. You are transforming red rows into green ones. That's impact.
Ivy: Anyway, I was so demoralized I started applying to random jobs on LinkedIn at 3 am in my pajamas.
Morrie: Bold. That's when the algorithm is most empathetic.
Ivy: One of them replied. In Dutch. I don't speak Dutch.
Morrie: That never stopped the British from colonizing...
Ivy: They scheduled an interview. I panicked. So I googled "Dutch business culture" and watched a video of a guy aggressively eating raw herring. I showed up, butchered the pronunciation of the company name, and accidentally told the VP I was "horny to learn."
Morrie: ...and did you get the job?
Ivy: I start next month.
Morrie: Serendipity, baby. Powered by insomnia and smelly fish videos.

***

Practical exercises

To practice the key ideas discussed in this chapter, work on the following three actionable exercises:

Serendipity journaling
Activity: Keep a daily or weekly journal where you note any unexpected events and meetings you attend, or ideas that come to mind. Reflect on how these could lead to new opportunities or learning paths in your consulting career.
Objective: To develop an awareness of the *positive exposure to randomness*, and learn to see value in unplanned encounters and experiences.

Diverse project sampling
Activity: Seek involvement in diverse projects within your firm, especially those beyond your expertise, including internal practice development work. Identify skills you would like to acquire and, to practice them, volunteer for attending client pitches, joining a cross-functional team, or shadowing colleagues from different departments.
Objective: To build a diverse portfolio of experiences, akin to *career door openers*, that broaden your skillset and increase your exposure to serendipitous opportunities.

Calculated randomness in networking
Activity: Every month, attend new events or network outside your field. Engage in tech meetups, exciting seminars, or casual coffees. Follow up with new contacts by sharing articles, asking thoughtful questions, or suggesting a catch-up call to discuss a mutual interest.

Objective: To practice *calculated randomness* in networking, expanding your personal and professional network beyond the usual circles.

Wear influence, and become the one others chase

There is an old Italian saying, one of those obscure, half-forgotten proverbs muttered by old fishermen in crumbling seaside towns, that goes: "Only an idiot casts his net in a storm. The smart man lets the fish jump in". To be precise, "idiot" is the clean version; the original is less indulgent. Now, I have no idea if any fisherman has actually said this, but my *nonno* (my grandpa, for the ones of you that don't speak Italian) certainly did, and that is what matters.

My grandfather was in the *Guardia di Finanza*, the Italian Fiscal Police. He was stationed in Gallipoli, a little town in Puglia, right at the heel of the Italian boot, that no American tourist could have placed on a map back then. Today, it is packed with sunburnt New Yorkers trying to *live like the locals*, but in his time, it was a quiet fishing hub where the real business happened out of sight (cash, catch, and quiet favors changing hands). Nonno had seen enough fishy accounting (literal and figurative) to know that the real business of the sea happened under the table. Occasionally, a crate or two of *unofficial* seafood made it past the controls. Let us just say that some nights, his dinner plate looked a little too good for a government salary, with my nonna doing out-of-hours work cooking mussels and swordfish.

One of his favorite stories was about a fisherman named Vincenzo, a man too lazy to chase anything: not a fish, not a woman, not even a tax declaration. While the other fishermen were out at dawn, throwing their nets with the desperation of men who needed to make rent, Vincenzo had a different strategy. He sat back in his boat, lit a cigarette, and let the tide do the work. Some called him a fool, others, a genius. One day, while the rest of the fleet was out chasing tuna with military precision, a violent gust of wind overturned a small fishing boat nearby, sending a crate of prized red shrimp tumbling into the sea. The shrimp, stunned by the fall, floated helplessly on the surface. Without moving an inch, Vincenzo watched as the tide carried the entire crate straight into his boat. He barely had to extend his arm. He sailed back to shore, sold the shrimp for a small fortune (the Italian lira back then was worth something), and spent the next two weeks drinking espresso and philosophizing about fate.

What does this have to do with networking? Everything. Most people treat networking like those frantic fishermen: casting their nets, chasing opportunities, filling their calendars with desperate one-on-ones. The actual game is about positioning yourself so that opportunities come to you. You want to be Vincenzo, sitting in the right place at the right time, letting the tide do the work.

This is what I call *Upside-Down Networking*: not chasing but attracting, not seeking permission but being invited. It is the art of being in rooms where you have no business being, simply because people need you there. Traditional networking is all about reaching out, making connections, and seeking advice. The method is tried and true, but you are constantly chasing something that you are not even sure is there. Those are the key verbs here: *to seek* and *to chase.*

The first lesson discussed in the book is: "Serendipity strikes those who seek it."

What if, instead of *You* going to *Them*, we focus on creating opportunities for *Them* to come to *You*? This is the fundamental principle of Upside-Down Networking.

A bad lawyer can be a good teacher

You do not need to be Italian or a literary aficionado to appreciate *I Promessi Sposi* (*The Betrothed*), a cornerstone of literature written by Alessandro Manzoni in the 19th century. Think of it as a soap opera wrapped in a philosophical treatise, with the occasional moralizing flourish thrown in for good measure. The plot twists are some incredible stuff that makes *Game of Thrones* look like a tepid office drama. Among the dozens of memorable characters, there is a young man named Renzo Tramaglino, your classic decent, hardworking fellow (a silk weaver, to be precise), with all the naivety of a man who believes the world is fair just because he plays by the rules. He is deeply in love with Lucia, a girl of equal virtue, and the two are engaged to be married. As you might expect, *Fate* (in the form of a powerful local lord named Don Rodrigo) has other plans. Don Rodrigo, driven by nothing but petty lust and his sense of unearned privilege, decides he wants Lucia for himself. Because, of course, he does.

When I was in high school studying *I Promessi Sposi*, I already had a favorite character: the *Azzeccagarbugli* (more on him in a second). I did not quite know why I found him so compelling back then, but something about his cunning duplicity was oddly fascinating. I definitely did not know back then that my future professional life would bring me face to face with so many people who seemed to have walked straight out of Manzoni's pages. Azzeccagarbugli literally means "the entangler of problems," which should tell you everything you need to know about him.

He was a lawyer, think of him as the Renaissance version of Saul Goodman from *Better Call Saul* or *Breaking Bad*, the specimen of legal shark who would have slapped a cheesy slogan on a billboard if only the printing press had been widespread. Saul Goodman, at least, is somewhat charming and overtly transactional about his dubious services. Azzeccagarbugli, on the other hand, wraps himself in a pretense of scholarly respectability. This is a man who has built his reputation not by solving problems, but by muddying them up just enough to bill you for clarification. He thrives in the murky waters of complexity, a bottom-feeder feasting on the confusion of others. Like Saul Goodman's shadier dealings, Azzeccagarbugli's true skill lies in his ability to manipulate the letter of the law, twist it, and, most importantly, make it seem like only he has the key to unlocking its intricacies. He is that lawyer who reads the fine print not to interpret it, but to invent new layers of fine print. Azzeccagarbugli is a helpful metaphor for every incompetent consultant who pretends to solve problems while actually deepening them, spewing recommendations designed more to impress than to work, creating the illusion of expertise rather than delivering real value. Azzeccagarbugli's power is the appearance of knowledge, not knowledge itself. And when you try to approach him with an earnest plea for help, like Renzo does, he sniffs out your desperation and uses it to push you away. The more desperate you are, the more useless he becomes.

That is the danger of chasing influence rather than attracting it.

You run headlong into the Azzeccagarbuglis of the world, those so-called *experts* whose leading talent is crafting elaborate façades of competence, built on the shaky foundation of their own self-interest. And when you come at them with the wrong approach, their power over you only grows. Renzo, being the straightforward, trusting soul that he is, marches into Azzeccagarbugli's lair with some money in hand and the desperate belief that justice is something you can buy with a few coins and a bit of honest pleading. He lays out his case, that Don Rodrigo is preventing his rightful marriage to Lucia, while Azzeccagarbugli, sensing money on the table, initially plays the role of the sympathetic counselor. He gives Renzo the impression that justice is indeed a purchasable commodity. And Renzo, blissfully ignorant, buys into it. When Azzeccagarbugli realizes that Renzo's opponent is Don Rodrigo, a man of wealth and the kind of local influence that makes lawyers either very rich or very dead, he changes his tune. The man's demeanor shifts from feigned righteousness to panic. He pushes Renzo out of his office like a rotting fish being tossed from a fancy dinner table, all the while murmuring half-baked excuses about how he cannot possibly take on such a case. His moral backbone is as flexible as wet spaghetti.

The lesson is crystal clear: Renzo approached the situation all wrong. He thought that simply having a grievance and waving it around like a child with a toy sword would make people rally to his cause. He tried to force his way into the favor of a powerful man, not realizing that the act of trying too hard was itself a signal of weakness. Renzo's desperation was written all over his face, and Azzeccagarbugli picked up on it immediately. Renzo's failure is the classic mistake of believing that action alone will bring results. He reaches out, casts his net wide, and ends up empty-handed. Azzeccagarbugli's office explains the wrong form of networking: rooms where your desperation makes you disposable.

The principle of *Upside-Down Networking* is the opposite. It is about becoming the persona that people like Azzeccagarbugli would feel compelled to listen to, rather than shoving your problem under their noses with the false confidence of someone who thinks persistence is a substitute for positioning.

Manzoni understood human nature with the cold clarity of a surgeon operating without anesthesia. If you try to bludgeon your way into influence, you will find yourself at the mercy of the Azzeccagarbuglis that gravitate around you today. However, if you understand how to position yourself so that influence seeks you out, then you will be the one whose advice is sought rather than discarded.

Time for a personal story.

Traditions in Wimbledon

It was 2009, and the financial crisis hit companies like a sledgehammer. The consulting firm I was working for was no exception. Budgets were cut, projects were canned, and I was a semi-junior consultant, wondering how to make my mark. I was working on a complex engagement for a multinational insurance company, stationed in Wimbledon, where the only thing more traditional than the All England Club's dress code was the thinking of one particular workstream lead. My boss, the program director, had placed his trust in this old-school British gentleman, a man nearing retirement with a frame that suggested a lifelong appreciation for proper Yorkshire pudding. He was unassuming, polite, and as conservative in his business thinking as in his taste for tea.

Meanwhile, I had niche experience from a previous engagement in a similar context and stumbled upon a creative solution to a business process issue, one that had completely eluded him and his team. Yes, everyone else had overlooked it, but I had solved a similar problem before, so I was confident in my reasoning. It was a bit like watching an old-school tennis coach insist on wooden rackets while I had a carbon-fiber one in my hands: respect for tradition is great, but sometimes you just need to update your grip and swing (apologies, but I couldn't resist making a tennis joke here!)

I was convinced that, as the project progressed, these minor issues I had uncovered would become irreversible and end up with us, as a consultancy, unable to deliver the outcome we had promised to the client. Such a claim from a junior consultant like me was a bit cocky, especially with that narrow-minded guy at the helm, but I was not one to lock my ideas away and pretend I did not see anything. I packaged my insight into a few intelligent slides and dropped them casually with the program leadership during lunch.

I didn't ask for a pat on the back.

I said something like, "Hey, I discovered this information that might be useful for us, and maybe we should discuss going in this particular direction regarding the project instead of continuing with the current approach."

Then, nonchalantly but still unassuredly, I returned to my poorly crafted ham sandwich, which I had just bought from the corner shop run by two Iranian immigrants claiming to serve "Italian panini" (oooh, the stories from that place).

In less than a week, I was invited to a strategy meeting with top-level execs to discuss my findings and concerns.

This is the magic of Upside-Down Networking. I offered something valuable (a fresh perspective, a new approach, unique insights) without asking for anything in return. This conscious action opened doors to rooms I had never thought I could have access to before.

You will be amazed at the lengths Directors and Partners in your firm will go to get your opinion, value your ideas, and ultimately help you climb the corporate ladder at a pace you didn't know was possible. And you know why they would give a hoot about you? It all boils down to a combination of self-interest and the inherent dynamics of consulting.

How to make Upside-Down Networking work

Even if you know nothing about consulting, you must know this: your senior leaders have a lot on their plates. They manage complex projects, navigate client relationships, and juggle internal politics, all while keeping an eye on the top and bottom lines.

Corporate leaders have their KPIs, performance metrics and career ambitions: they are all swamped and going through a mild midlife crisis.

When someone filled with youthful vigor and curiosity comes along offering genuinely valuable perspectives that can improve the outcomes they are concerned with, you can bet their sweet spreadsheets, they listen!

For example, suppose you have helped identify a strategy to increase client retention or revealed an opportunity for revenue growth. In that case, you are not just another consultant: you have evolved into *an asset* (more on this idea later).

Consulting is not (should not be) *quid pro quo*: at its core, it is about forming long-term, meaningful relationships. Your senior leaders understand this.

If you were to take one thing from this reading experience, take this: *Play the long game.* Today, you are helping them nail a key project. Tomorrow, they might recommend you for a senior role or an exciting new venture. That's how you have to think.

In consulting, your reputation is your currency.

If you are the one that Partners start seeking out for advice, that reputation begins to compound: word travels fast in most firms. Soon, other influential people will start noticing you, which is when you have to leverage your newfound reputation to your advantage.

As Benjamin Franklin said, "An investment in knowledge pays the best interest." When Partners invest in you by seeking your advice and insights, they also invest in their futures. It's a win-win.

Reminder: Traditional networking is about reaching out, casting your net wide, and hoping that something latches on. Upside-Down Networking draws people in by transforming you into the premium fish catch that attracts the seasoned fishermen: your bosses and leaders. It's about providing something so valuable that they can't help but seek you out.

So, how to make it work?

First, you've got to have something your leaders want, something they only knew they needed once they saw it. The crux of what they usually want is to save time and money. Be proactive. If you suggest something as basic as the structure of the slide or as advanced as a technical opinion on operational efficiency, as a Partner, I want to hear it as long as it's helpful.

Even if you are worried your insight is not particularly clever, say it anyway: a good firm and a good boss will encourage that. And if you are not in a good firm and do not have a good boss, well, that is still valuable information, because it tells you something essential about your environment. If speaking up gets you sidelined or ignored, then the problem is the organizational culture. A culture that penalizes candor breeds mediocrity. Over time, you will find yourself self-censoring, second-guessing, and slowly detaching from the work. That is not just bad for your career: it is corrosive to your sense of agency. So, take the hint. Either shield yourself and find allies who get it, or start quietly building your way out. The longer you stay in a place that punishes thoughtfulness, the harder it becomes to believe your thoughts are worth sharing at all.

Take a look back at the scenario I gave earlier. I dropped a nugget of gold to my bosses that they could work on to rescue the program for a critical client. Presenting this information, which I knew was valuable and urgent, casually in a conversation created an environment where my leadership started thinking of me as a go-to guy for fresh perspectives.

The second factor is subtlety. The art of Upside-Down Networking lies in not making it evident that you are trying to get their attention. You do not have to send calendar invites for one-on-ones or spam their inbox with articles you think they should read. Instead, you integrate your value-adds into existing channels such as team meetings, shared reports, and informal lunches. You drop a groundbreaking idea as if it were a casual chit-chat.

The third element is patience and consistency. One brilliant idea won't make you the go-to person for your Partner, but consistently delivering actionable insights will. Each time you bring something fresh, you are laying another brick in a path that leads straight to you. Over time, that path becomes a runway, and your leadership team will start landing on it sooner than you expect, seeking your input and advice.

The beauty of Upside-Down Networking is that it's a two-way street. Yes, Partners start to seek you out, but in the process, they also become more accessible to *you*. This opens new doors for you to learn directly from the people who have already done what you want to do, and have the experience you need to help you grow faster.

Do you know who understood the power of attracting opportunity? Sun Tzu. The man was not some philosophical daydreamer writing pretty words sitting on an ergonomic chair like yours truly. He was a ruthless Chinese military strategist from the 5th century BC who literally wrote the book on winning. *The Art of War* is about crushing your enemies with precision, cunning, sheer audacity, and his words still echo today: "Opportunities multiply as they are seized." What he meant was simple:

action begets action. When you create value, people notice. And once people start noticing, more opportunities flow your way. You build momentum, and, in consulting, momentum is everything. Without it, you are just another anonymous drone, clicking away at slides like a caffeinated hamster on a wheel.

Upside-Down Networking operates on the principle of *pull rather than push*. It is how you get your consulting career out of the slow lane and into the fast track.

Of course, it doesn't have to stop there.

Once you start seeing quantifiable growth in your career, you can apply the fundamentals more broadly outside your firm. Imagine attracting interest from potential clients, industry thought leaders, and even competitors. As I said, words travel fast around here.

It's a relatively simple shift in strategy, but its effects can ripple out, causing a seismic change in your career trajectory.

The next time you ponder how to get ahead, forget the old playbook. Flip the script. Don't be the fisherman. Be the prized fish.

***

Vignette

Morrie is eating a tuna sandwich in his office when Ivy walks in with a bunch of thick reports and her laptop. Morrie continues eating his sandwich and scrolling through a spreadsheet without paying any attention to Ivy.

Ivy: Do you know what I want in my current career?
Morrie: You can't get a promotion with 1 year of experience, Ivy. We have gone over this.
Ivy: Yes, yes. I KNOW. Consulting has a clear career trajectory; I was only half asleep in the orientation program. I want something better.
Morrie [finishes his sandwich and looks up]: You have my attention. Shoot.
Ivy: I wanna be in the room where *it* happens.
Morrie [with a proud look]: Define *it*.
Ivy: I mean, *it*. You know the *it*. I don't just want to be another junior consultant in the eyes of my seniors, you know.
Morrie: First of all, apart from the strategic decisions, all you are missing are soccer trash-talking and hair transplant updates.
Ivy: So, when is your appointment? *[chuckles]*
Morrie: What you want is to become an *asset*. Start offering your unique perspective that helps Partners.
Ivy: Actually, my father is a hair transplant surg--
Morrie: No, gosh! About client satisfaction and revenue increase. Word travels fast among executives. If you are valuable to them, they are accessible to you.
Ivy: I seriously think I would be good at soccer.

***

Practical exercises

To practice the key ideas discussed in this chapter, work on the following three actionable exercises:

Insight sharing initiative

Activity: Launch a semi-regular newsletter or email list within your team to share insights, innovative solutions, or summaries of compelling articles in your industry. Remember, the aim is to benefit your peers and not boast about your efforts or knowledge.
Objective: This exercise cultivates offering value without seeking validation. Position yourself as a thought leader and go-to person for fresh ideas, following the *Upside-Down Networking* approach.

Problem-solving challenge

Activity: Identify a recurring issue in your current project or firm processes. Ponder over the problem after work hours, trying to find a creative solution. Share your insight with your project manager casually, framing it as something low-key that might be helpful.
Objective: The aim is to take initiative and showcase proactive problem-solving. Addressing concerns overlooked by others boosts your visibility and value within the team.

Informal networking moments

Activity: Engage in casual chats with your peers and clients. Make a habit of engaging in conversations during breaks, elevator rides, or through virtual coffee meetings. Share something interesting you learned recently, or seek opinions on non-confidential work topics.

Objective: Build genuine relationships outside work to subtly showcase interests, knowledge, and value via informal interactions.

SPEAK LIKE YOU BELONG, OR BE TREATED LIKE BACKGROUND NOISE

Your words are the vehicle for your ideas, the bridge between thought and action, strategy and implementation.

It is easy to talk a good game, but in consulting, once you master your language, you set yourself on a path of influence and opportunities.

Think about it: every sector has its language, a matrix of terminology, frameworks, and acronyms. This is not jargon for the sake of gatekeeping; it is shorthand for complex concepts.

For instance, if you are working with a financial services client and casually mention *EBITDA* without hesitation or fumbling, you speak their language. You demonstrate that you understand their world, which also means you can build trust.

Let's take it a step further.

Charlie Munger, the legendary investor and partner of Warren Buffett, once said: "I think that every time you see the word EBITDA, you should substitute the words *bullshit earnings*."

Imagine quoting Munger while discussing EBITDA with your clients: they will probably think of you as a curious youngster passionate about the subject and with a good sense of humor. They will also see something more important: you are not just parroting industry lingo, but you have a *point of view* and are not afraid to engage with the ideas behind the words.

That is what sets a great consultant apart from a walking corporate dictionary. Confidence does not come from memorizing frameworks, but from understanding them deeply enough to challenge them. When you quote Munger's sharp take on EBITDA, you show that you know the term, and signal that you *think* about it. You are inviting discussion, maybe even a little debate. And that is where absolute trust is built. Clients do not just want someone who knows their industry's language, they want someone who can speak it with personality.

Consulting is full of professionals who are fluent in business jargon but empty of conviction (some call them *the empty suits*), but the ones who stand out are those who can wield language, not just repeat it.

What you say influences the perception that other people have about you. Every word you utter and the terms you employ are subtle indicators of your competence and aura: when you speak the lingo fluently, you assert your expertise and yourself. And if you want to join an elite club, you must know the exclusive handshake for the doors to open.

There is only one caveat: overuse or, worse, misuse the vocabulary, and you will be pegged as a try-hard or a phony.

How do you avoid that? A way to master business language is through *contextual learning*, the process of understanding and absorbing information concerning the specific situation in which it is applied.

It's not enough to simply memorize facts or formulae: one must grasp the relationships between those facts and the environment in which they are used. This is especially relevant for consultants, as our value is not measured in what we know but in applying what we know to solve unique problems. For consultants at the start of their careers, diving into contextual learning means actively relating every piece of new information to real-world scenarios.

Consider the following example.

You learn about a business framework like the popular *Porter's Five Forces.*

Rather than just memorizing the components, you must examine how each force plays out in the specific industry you are consulting for. You should look at current market dynamics, recent case studies, and even news articles discussing trends affecting that sector.

Applying new knowledge to real-world scenarios is highly beneficial beyond what's immediately apparent: it enables you to remember. There is a reason stories are passed down through generations while facts are usually forgotten.

Stories stick. So, when you wrap a new piece of information in the narrative of a project, it embeds itself in your memory.

As you grow into your consultant role, you will realize that contextual learning makes you adaptable. The skillset that serves you on a project in financial services may be a challenging fit for healthcare. Still, the core competencies you would have developed (analytical thinking, communication, or project management) are easily transferable.

Solving problems is at the heart of what you do. With each new piece of information, you sharpen your ability to predict patterns, anticipate potential pitfalls, and design strategies that proactively address those challenges before they fully emerge.

Cultivating this contextual wisdom is an active process.

Dive deep into case studies that resonate with your work: do not just read but dissect them.

What would you have done differently? Why did a particular strategy work? Simulate these scenarios, role-play the dynamics, and engage in critical post-project reflections. This is how theoretical jargon evolves into *understanding*.

Through contextual learning, you will bridge the gap between theory and action and develop a specific *wisdom*, a consulting intuition that guides you when there are no precedents to follow.

One of my former bosses, a towering 50-year-old Dutchman with the demeanor of a CFO and the bluntness of a man who had no time for fluff, once told me that the right way to interpret our profession is to become a *practical consultant*. This guy saw the world in two colors: green, when things were going well, and red, when they were not. There was no yellow, no shades of nuance, just the cold, hard logic of numbers. Trust me, you wanted to stay in his green zone. A direct man, because he was Dutch after all, he had a great sense of business and an even greater love for his Excel sheets.

He could size up a situation faster than most people could open their laptops, and if he liked you (like he liked me), life was good. If he did not, well... let us just say, some people learned to dread his emails. When he told me the most effective consultants are practical ones, he was right, of course. You must switch from a theoretically knowledgeable consultant to a pragmatically wise one, and, once you have the proper understanding and knowledge, your focus should quickly turn to *how* to communicate that effectively.

Let's see what can be done there.

Actionable tactics for linguistic mastery

With the right techniques, your communication skills can improve rapidly, and compound over time. You can, of course, go very deep into each of the following ideas if you are interested, but reflecting on what you are going to read next, and doing the exercises at the end of the chapter, will give you a head start. Note that reading the theory will help you, sure, but only to a certain extent, because practice is 90% of this game.

Most people think communication is about talking. It is not. It is about control: controlling the room, controlling the tempo, and controlling how your ideas are received.

The best way to gain control is to listen first. Sit in meetings and steal phrases. Watch how senior leaders frame their points, the exact words they use to persuade or deflect. Ever notice how a Partner never says, "This is a bad idea"? Instead, they say, "I am struggling to see the value in this." That phrasing softens the critique while making their skepticism clear. Pick up these subtleties. Mimic them, and do it with intent. Copying blindly makes you sound like an AI-generated consultant, one that people will quietly mock in team chats and never take seriously.

Use words that mean exactly what you intend. Do not say *cash flow* when you mean *liquidity*. Do not say *synergy* when you mean *overlap*. I once watched a consultant getting grilled for five minutes because he said, "We need to improve the operational processes" without specifying *which* operations or *what* efficiency metric. If you ramble, you are forgotten. If you are sharp, you are remembered.

After every meeting, replay the key moments.

Did you make sense? Did people nod along, or did they squint like they were deciphering some random guy from Connecticut trying to speak French? Ask someone you trust: "Did that land?" If not, why? Maybe you used too much jargon. Maybe your argument had a gap. Identify the problem and fix it.

If you want to truly master communication, teach. Nothing forces clarity like explaining a concept to others. Lead a meeting. Write something down. I once had to train a group of new hires on the step-by-step business process to outline a credit card payment. I thought I knew the topic inside out, until I had to break it down in plain English. Every small gap in my understanding became obvious because teaching forces you to organize your thoughts, sharpening your communication.

Your pauses, rhythm, and presence fill in the gaps between the words.

Great speakers know that *how* you deliver a message is just as important as *what* you say, especially when the news is bad. The best communicators *command* attention: they slow down, control their tone, and let silence carry weight. Contrast that with someone who stumbles through a problematic message, voice cracking, words spilling out in a rush. One leaves the audience reassured, even in crisis. The other leaves them uneasy.

Let's look at two moments in history: one when a speaker *owned* the room and one when he simply *filled* it.

Churchill VS Nixon

On June 4, 1940, Winston Churchill stood before the British Parliament to address a nation in crisis. France was collapsing under the Nazi onslaught, and Britain faced the terrifying possibility of invasion. The mood was grim. Fear was spreading. Britain needed reassurance.

Churchill delivered it with *masterful control*. His voice was low and steady, carrying the weight of history. He paced his words deliberately, making sure each phrase landed with impact. His sentences were rhythmic, designed to *be remembered*:

> "We shall fight on the beaches, we shall fight on the landing grounds, we shall fight in the fields and in the streets, we shall fight in the hills; we shall never surrender."

The repetition of "we shall fight" built momentum, giving his words a sense of inevitability. He paused strategically, letting the silence *amplify* his message. There was no filler or rambling, but *pure resolve*.

Churchill delivered a speech and *owned* the moment. His voice, pacing, and delivery worked together to project strength and certainty. Even as Britain faced its darkest hour, he made people *believe*.

Fast forward to 1973, and move across the pond, to the United States of America. Embroiled in the Watergate scandal, Richard Nixon was fighting for his political survival. Public trust was crumbling, and he needed to reassure the nation. Instead, he did the opposite.

During a press conference in Florida, Nixon addressed the scandal head-on. But instead of controlling the room, he sounded defensive and desperate. His voice was uneven, alternating between forced confidence and nervous agitation. Then, he uttered the infamous lines:

> "I want to say this to the American people. I have never profited, never profited from public service. I have earned every cent. And in all of my years of public life, I have never obstructed justice. People have got to know whether or not their President is a crook. Well, I am not a crook."

His tone betrayed his words! He spoke too quickly, as if trying to *outrun* the accusations. Instead of exuding control, he sounded like a man *pleading for innocence*. The phrase "I am not a crook" should have reassured people; instead, it became the headline, the joke, the proof that he was losing his grip.

Unlike Churchill, who let pauses build power, Nixon rushed through his points, making him sound jittery. His voice rose at odd moments, signaling unease rather than confidence. The more he spoke, the worse it got.

The result was that the press and public did not hear *reassurance*. They heard *guilt*.

Now, consider body language.

As a consultant, your posture, gestures, and even micro-expressions affect how your message is received. Before you even say a word, people form an opinion of your confidence and competence. The way you enter a room, the firmness of your handshake, the assuredness with which you click through a presentation: all these elements script the perception of your competence.

There is an old story (maybe a legend?) I was told by a friend of mine about a Senior Partner at his firm (the M in MBB...) who had an unconventional way of evaluating candidates. He did not obsess over GPAs. He skimmed through résumés. He barely glanced at case interview results. Instead, he watched *how* candidates walked into the room. If they entered hesitantly, with their shoulders slightly hunched, scanning the space like they were waiting for permission to exist, he would mentally check out before they even spoke. But he would lean in and listen if they walked in with measured steps, shook hands firmly, and sat down like they *belonged* at the table. He did this because he knew something that even competent consultants often forget: *before you convince clients of your intelligence, you must first convince them of your conviction.*

The best ideas fall flat if the consultant looks unsure, but even average ones *can* land if delivered with confidence. It is not fair, I know, but it is how the world works. Clients do not just buy solutions: they buy *certainty*. If you do not sound certain about your ideas, why should they be? This leads me to tone.

The tonal quality of your voice carries the essence of emotion and intent. The voice is a powerful instrument: play it wisely. A confident and level tone can convey authority and reassure a client, while a waver may sow doubt: gravitas is a natural and tangible skill to learn.

The enthusiasm in your voice can ignite excitement about a new idea; conversely, a mono-tone can suck the energy out of the most compelling proposal. Watch an entrepreneur pitching their start-up: the best ones do not just rattle off numbers but inject controlled excitement. The worst ones might have the next trillion-dollar idea, but no one will care if they present it like a tax accountant reading a compliance manual.

Timing in communication is your strategic ally.

You must know when to interject with a key insight or when to pause for emphasis, allowing your words to sink in. You must understand how to pace your dialogue to match the rhythm of the conversation, ensuring your input is timely and impactful. Like a comedian mastering the punchline, the consultant must master the art of delivery to maximize influence.

And, as we just discussed contextual learning, we can't ignore context, of course!

Context is the window that frames the relevance of the painting your language creates. The exact phrase can have different meanings in a boardroom full of C-suite executives versus a casual chat with peers. The ability to *read the room*, be it a client's office, a video call, even a chance encounter at an airport lounge, requires you to adapt your language smartly.

Consider the infamous story of Gerald Ratner, the former CEO of the UK jewelry chain Ratners Group. At its peak, Ratners was a retail empire, with over 2,000 stores and millions in revenue. Then, in a single moment of spectacular misjudgment, he destroyed it all.

In April 1991, Ratner was giving a speech to the Institute of Directors, a high-profile business audience (you can still find the video of the speech on YouTube). Instead of the usual polished corporate remarks, he decided to go for humor. He joked that one of Ratners' best-selling products was "total crap." He went further, saying that a pair of their earrings was "cheaper than a prawn sandwich but probably wouldn't last as long."

The audience laughed. The press did not. Within days, the tabloids had splashed Ratner's words everywhere. Customers fled, and the company's valuation plummeted by over £500 million. This loss represented a drop of approximately 80% in the company's market value by the end of 1991. Within a year, Ratner had lost his business, his fortune, and his reputation. All because he forgot one thing: *context.* That same joke might have killed it in a private dinner among close friends, but in front of journalists, investors, and industry leaders, it was the equivalent of suicide. Most of us as consultants do not deal in jewelry, but we deal in perception, and we must learn how to speak with a balance of confidence and awareness.

Once you master the art of effective communication, which is just good storytelling at its core, you can craft an experience around your message that is fluid with your audience. Thus, communication evolves into an instrument of persuasion and connection.

Mastering storytelling, like any other skill, requires time and patience.

Getting comfortable with the complex arrangement of tone, timing, body language, and context is quite similar to moving to a new city (I know something about it because I have lived in nine different places on four different continents.)

You spend days or months figuring out your favorite route to walk, regular places to eat or have drinks, and a desperate amount of time making new friends. Eventually, navigating the transport system becomes second nature and, before you know it, the local pizzeria owner knows your name, makes your usual *Capricciosa* as soon as you walk in, and gets you a complimentary *limoncello* at the end of the evening (true story).

What's important is to actually walk around, and invest in yourself for the long haul.

But I work from home!

I know, I know. Some of you out there are complaining that much of what I said so far is not really applicable to you because you Work From Home.

My answer is, "it depends" (after all, am I or am I not a consultant?!).

Let me explain. The shift to remote meetings in consulting has thrown everyone into a new reality where words and expressions are everything. The absence of a shared physical space means the nuances of communication are so much more important. Every twitch of an eyebrow, every slight raise of the voice, becomes amplified and scrutinized through the cold lens of a webcam.

Think about it. You are trying to project authority and insight through a tiny screen while your daughter is listening to Taylor Swift full volume, your cat decides now is the perfect time to reenact parkour championships off-camera, your neighbor's dog is losing its mind over a rogue lizard, and your dog is suddenly howling like he just discovered his ancestors were wolves. It is a fucking mess, but you are expected to look like the calmest person in the Teams call. Welcome to the new arena of consulting: the digital colosseum. You'd better show up ready to fight.

The rules have changed, but the game is still the same: you need to command the room, even if the room is a bunch of tiny squares on a monitor. In a remote setting, body language is reduced to the space between your shoulders and the top of your head. Your new gladiator weapons are your facial expressions, eye contact, and gestures. Lean forward slightly to show interest, nod thoughtfully to indicate you get it. It is all about communicating presence without actually being present. Your voice now does the heavy lifting that your whole body used to do. It has to convey authority, warmth, clarity, and energy all at once. The way you inflect, the pauses you take, the emphasis you throw at the right words matter more than ever. If you sound bored, uninterested, or distracted, they will assume you are bored, uninterested, or distracted. Your voice has to carry the weight of the message *and* the vibe you are trying to project.

I will give you an example. In 1932, Franklin D. Roosevelt gave his famous *Fireside Chats* addresses over the radio. America was in the Great Depression, and he needed to calm a nation drowning in fear. The man used nothing but his voice to make people feel like he was speaking directly to them from their living rooms. He painted words with empathy and authority so effectively that it felt like he was reaching through the radio waves and patting people on the back. And he did it from a microphone, not a stage. Now, imagine pulling off that level of connection in your virtual meetings!

Timing in remote meetings is a dance you have to master. There is the lag, the awkward silences, and the endless "Sorry, you go first" interruptions. You need to read the room when it is just a collection of pixelated faces. Learning to pause at the right moment, acknowledging others with subtle head movements, or even gracefully interrupting when the moment calls for it: all of it counts. If you do not master this, your words will be swallowed by the digital void.

The context of communication in remote settings is also about creating a clean, professional digital presence. Your backdrop, your lighting, your camera angle are fundamental. If you are trying to come across as an authority but your background looks like a scout camping tent situation, good luck.

Of course, technical blunders will happen. They happen to everyone. Some time ago, a Partner I was having a call with, accidentally unmuted himself while cursing at his malfunctioning laptop (no, it wasn't me, but it could have been me!). Instead of panicking, he laughed it off, joked about modern technology being a "beautiful nightmare" and moved on. It was brilliant because it was human. Acknowledging imperfections in this environment makes you more relatable, not less.

This new era of consulting communication is about embracing constraints and making them work for you. You will never have the same presence as you would in person, but that just means you need to make every word, gesture, and interaction count even more. The *gift of gab* in consulting is no longer just about eloquence and charm. It is about *impact* and the ability to deliver your message with clarity, empathy, and precision, whether sitting across the table from someone or appearing in a 3x3 cm window (that is 1.18 inches if that's what you do) on their laptop. It's a potent cocktail of empathy, intellect, strategy, and, yes, a bit of theater.

Master that, and you will be playing the game at a higher level than most of your competitors even realize.

***

Vignette

Morrie is lazily flipping through a thick industry magazine titled "Consulting Quarterly." Ivy bursts in, holding a notepad covered in scribbles and acronyms.

Ivy: Okay, hear me out. *"EBITDA, KPI, ESG, RFP, synergies, boiling the ocean"*. I am learning *all* the lingo now. I am basically fluent.
Morrie [without looking up]: Congratulations. You are now a walking corporate fortune cookie.
Ivy: Come on. Knowing the language means credibility, right?
Morrie: No. *Understanding* the language means credibility. Parroting it means you are two conference calls away from becoming an "empty suit."
Ivy [defensive]: But if I drop the right terms at the right time, I sound smart.
Morrie: You do not get paid to *sound* smart. You get paid to *be* useful. Big difference. Quoting EBITDA makes you fluent. Quoting Munger on EBITDA makes you dangerous.
Ivy [scribbling furiously]: Right. Be fluent, but have a point of view. No corporate fortune cookie. Got it.
Morrie [finally looking up]: And remember: Language is not there to show you are part of the club. It is there to *build your own.*

Ivy pauses, then smiles slowly. Morrie tosses the magazine onto the desk, revealing the headline: "Top Ten Phrases That Make You Sound Smarter." He rolls his eyes so hard it is practically audible.

***

Practical exercises

To practice the key ideas discussed in this chapter, work on the following three actionable exercises:

Contextual vocabulary building

Activity: Every week, research a new industry term, including its meaning, origin, and real-world application. Create a short presentation or a one-page summary of your learnings that includes an example of applications, and reflects on implications for your work.

Objective: To enhance industry language comprehension and communication skills. This activity enables continuous learning and practical application within projects. Also, it reinforces your understanding and ability to discuss these terms confidently and accurately.

Active listening and mimicry (with moderation)

Activity: During meetings, observe how experienced consultants and corporate leaders communicate. Note how they utilize language, structure arguments, and use metaphors. Reflect afterward, and incorporate these into your communication style authentically.

Objective: To enhance your listening skills and adapt effective communication strategies from seasoned professionals. This exercise encourages you to be mindful of your speech, and gradually refine your communication style, making it more impactful and authentic.

Simulated consulting scenarios

Activity: Set up regular consulting scenario-based roleplays with a group of mentors and peers. Each participant assumes a specific role and objective, practicing industry-specific language and confident delivery. After each session, offer constructive feedback to each other, focusing on language use, clarity of communication, and overall effectiveness.

Objective: To build confidence while using industry language effectively, adapting communication to diverse situations, and healthy reception of feedback.

REFLECT ON THYSELF, QUESTION EVERYONE ELSE

Have you ever received feedback that felt like a sucker punch to the guts?

Maybe it was in a team meeting where your manager disassembled your work like a watchmaker in reverse, except instead of putting it back together, they just left the pieces scattered on the table for everyone to see. Or maybe it arrived via email, an eloquent but unmistakable assassination of your competence, punctuated with phrases like "Let's rethink this approach" or "I have some concerns" (which, in consulting, is code for "This is shit").

Ouch, I know. It is painful.

In this chapter, I want to acknowledge the stricter side of a high-performance environment: the sharp edges, the sting of setbacks, the challenge of turning criticism into something constructive.

At the heart of it all, we have our friend, or foe, Ego.

Do not worry: Feeling hurt is natural, and I am not here to call you out for it. My point is that we all have an ego, and whether we like it or not, it serves a purpose. It cushions our self-image against the world's harsher realities, acting like the bumpers in a bowling alley, keeping us from veering entirely off track. But just like those bumpers, an overinflated ego can also distort our vision, making us blind to obstacles that lie ahead.

Even the most humble person is not immune to this: a successful implementation, a bit of positive feedback on a presentation... it does not take much to feel a surge of confidence! That in itself is not a problem. The real issue starts when we begin to believe we are beyond the pitfalls that trip up others, when we unconsciously see them as less capable than we are. You actually believe your myth and become the protagonist of a TED Talk in your head, a genius whose ideas arrive preordained from the heavens, immune to mortal error.

That is when Ego stops being a cushion and starts being a trap.

"I am too skilled, savvy, and gifted with innate talents to require caution or correction," or so our Ego convinces us. In consulting, the price of an inflated ego is astronomical. You stand to lose opportunities for personal growth, the trust of clients and team members, and, ultimately, the almighty revenue.

Criticism is your goddamn GPS. When you take a wrong turn, do you argue with Google Maps? No. (Well, maybe, but that is beside the point.) You re-route. You correct the course. Criticism is just another version of that, except instead of robotic turn-by-turn instructions, it comes in the form of your boss tearing your 50-slide deck apart in front of the entire team (more on this later).

The Stoics understood this long before consultants did. Marcus Aurelius, in his *Meditations*, talks about self-examination with ruthless honesty. He did not sugarcoat his mistakes and flaws. He dissected them and examined them like a scientist studying a specimen. You should do the same. Focus on what is in control of you: your personal growth, which derives from constant iteration and humility that enables you to change direction wherever necessary.

We must examine our failures, and the criticism they bring with an analytical detachment. That takes time to practice and execute. Once the waves of emotion settle down, a third-person (or Martian) perspective helps us take a more pragmatic and mechanical approach.

I have sat in meetings where my engagement leader torched my work like a medieval execution. Entire proposals, dozens of hours of effort, were dismissed in three words: "This needs rework."

Did I love it? Hell, no. Did I immediately want to throw my laptop out the window? Hell, yes.

But once the emotional dust settled, I realized something: every criticism was a cheat code, and each piece of feedback was a shortcut to a better outcome.

Once, I was working on a proposal with Jacob, my direct boss at the time. He was a former BCG Partner in the Sydney office, and a phenomenal storyteller. I had worked on this draft for a few days, and I was pretty confident he would be impressed by my output.

I had just started presenting my work to him and had yet to make it beyond page #4 when he made me stop. Jacob then made me print all the slides and lay them on the desk, rearranging the story with a frown on his face. He was making me change titles and telling me how to rewrite the content of each slide.

Jacob was the stereotypical Australian who looked like he had never spent a day indoors unless absolutely necessary. He had an athletic build, the lean, wiry frame of someone who had spent years swimming against the ocean's pull. Every morning, before most people had even hit snooze, he would dive into the surf at Maroubra, slicing through the cold water with the efficiency of a man who found clarity in movement. His skin was permanently sun-kissed, the lines around his eyes carved partly by age, partly by the relentless (and dangerous, I learned!) Aussie sun. He kept his black hair cropped short, more for practicality than style, and always dressed in a way that suggested he could bolt from a boardroom straight to the beach if given half a chance: crisp shirts with the sleeves rolled up, chinos that somehow never wrinkled, a pair of Oakley sunglasses carefully hiding in the pocket of his jacket, and a Garmin watch that had probably timed a few ocean swims before being worn to client meetings.

Even in the office, Jacob carried a quiet intensity, a presence that made you sit up straighter without him saying a word. When he worked, he worked with precision: no wasted motion or unnecessary fluff. Which is why, as he stood over my slides, reshuffling them like a puzzle with missing pieces, I realized my confidence had been premature.

Jacob was (and still is) a polite guy, so he gave me constructive criticism and did not call me an idiot. Any good boss should not, but I won't blame him if he thought of me as a nincompoop. After he was done explaining, I soaked in all the information, typed some notes, and made these learnings my standard for corporate storytelling going forward.

The skill of leveraging criticism for rapid skill enhancement lies in what I call *Radical Openness,* the willingness to put your ego aside and welcome criticism as a tool for growth.

To effectively practice Radical Openness, it's essential to separate *You, the person* from *You, the professional*. Yes, the criticism is aimed at your work, but that reflects your current skill level, not your worth as a human being.

You can, and likely will, become much more proficient at any specific skill: you just need to acknowledge that, at the very moment, you are receiving a piece of feedback because you are not there yet.

We all know this is easier said than done.

Steps for Radical Openness

You are a Roman senator in the court of Emperor Tiberius. You have presented your grand vision for economic reform eloquently and meticulously. It took you a while to prepare your deck, because PowerPoint is 2000 years away and, instead of slides, you had to rely on wax tablets and a very unimpressed scribe who kept rolling his eyes every time you asked for a *new version* ('pls fix' was already a thing back then). You have spent weeks refining your argument, consulting the finest minds in Rome, even slipping a few extra denarii to a particularly clever Greek philosopher for some last-minute insights. You stride into the Senate, chest puffed, voice steady, ready to unveil your magnum opus.

Tiberius listens, face unreadable. A long silence follows. You brace yourself for praise, perhaps even a sign of approval. Then, with the grace of a gladiator finishing off a wounded opponent, Tiberius leans forward and declines, in the most perfect Latin:

"This is the dumbest thing I have ever heard."

Now, you have two options.

Option one: You sulk, convince yourself Tiberius is a fool who does not appreciate your genius, and spend the rest of the evening muttering to yourself over wine. By the way, this is what your ego wants: self-pity, indignation, and, ultimately, stagnation.

Option two: You detach. You examine his words, not as a personal attack but as raw data. Perhaps your idea was flawed. Maybe it needs refinement. Possibly Tiberius, paranoid and erratic as he was, actually had a point. You take the feedback, tweak your approach, and live to present another day (hopefully without ending up exiled or poisoned).

This is the essence of Radical Openness: not clinging to your ego like a cheap toga but treating feedback as a strategic tool, something to be wielded, not feared.

Before we dive into the steps of Radical Openness, remember this. Every time your ego takes a hit, you are at a crossroads: you can become wiser or weaker. It's your choice.

Now, let us get to work.

- Start with self-awareness: The first hurdle is recognizing your ego. The ego is cunning: it prefers to avoid being spotted. To bypass it, one must engage in regular self-reflection. Take a few minutes daily to reflect on your actions, reactions, and emotions. You don't need to be a yogi; a quick check-in before bed or during your commute prepares you to receive feedback positively.

- Institutionalize feedback: Incorporate feedback as a regular part of your professional interactions. Whether during project post-mortems or in one-on-one sessions with colleagues or mentors, create spaces where feedback is not just welcome but expected. Regularly seek feedback, emphasizing and acknowledging its role in developing your skills. This keeps your ego in check and normalizes healthy criticism.

- Implement the "Three C's" Technique: When you receive criticism, filter it via the Clarify, Consider, and Choose framework. Firstly, *Clarify* and understand the feedback in simple terms, asking for examples if needed. Next, *Consider* its objective value. You don't have to like it, but strive to accept it and be "satisfied" with it, as one of my good leaders once told me. Finally, *Choose* how you want to react to the criticism. Appreciate your agency over future action; not all criticism is worth acting on.

- Active listening: When receiving criticism, practice listening actively. Nod your head, make eye contact, and even repeat the comments to confirm your understanding. Respect the input and avoid objecting to the feedback immediately, unless it is truly urgent.

- Fail forward: When you make mistakes, analyze them as data points for growth, not as indictments of your abilities. This shifts your mindset from fearing failure to embracing it as an inevitable step toward success. Every blunder is an opportunity to nail it the next time. If you can learn from your mistakes, you quickly become unstoppable.

- Engage in constructive self-talk: Your internal dialogue plays a critical role. When faced with criticism, avoid catastrophizing it. Swap out thoughts like, "I fucked up, I am terrible at this," with constructive self-talk like, "Okay, so that didn't go well. What can I learn here?". Remember that the more you accomplish, the more your confidence grows and the more you can achieve in the future.

- Celebrate small wins: Celebrate minor improvements as you implement changes based on feedback. The positive reinforcement encourages you to continue seeking out and acting on criticism, making it a virtuous growth cycle. A streak of small wins compounds into big wins over time.

"We are what we repeatedly do. Excellence, then, is not an act but a habit." Said *not* Aristotle (and honestly, I have no idea who did. Relevant pro tip: don't let your ego trip you up, and don't believe everything you read on the internet!).

Even if this was never said by Aristotle, the concept still stands. Do not file the learnings from criticism away for *future reference*. The point is to learn fast, act fast, fail fast, and improve fast. The faster the cycle, the more rapid your skill enhancement.

It is not wise to worship a dancer

An unfortunate mistake that some of the more seasoned consultants out there make is to confuse their years of experience with their ability to do the work. Experience *per se*, the mere passage of time, means *almost* nothing in consulting: what counts is whether you can produce the results you are requested to deliver, no matter what.

Consider this story, where an entire remote village once mistook a lightning strike for the blessing of a local *shaman*. During a drought, a bolt hit the parched earth right after the shaman had waved his feathered stick and danced in a circle. Rain followed. The villagers were awestruck. "The *shaman* brought water from the sky!" they proclaimed, before showering him with praise and a couple of goats. Next season, they built him a shrine and called him Rainmaker.

But when the next drought came, he danced till he collapsed, and the sky stayed dry. The truth, of course, is that he had no idea what had happened the first time: he was just in the right place, under the wrong cloud, at the right time.

Now, if a modern CEO walked into that village and heard the tale, he would be all excited, "He brought rain! Let's have him present a Brown Bag and lead a global practice at my consulting firm!" Nonsense.

Now what? You are going to hand over your pension and say, "Make it rain again, boss". You are going to trust the shaman's *experience*? This is the lie we keep telling ourselves: that past success undoubtedly means future brilliance, that because someone was dancing under freak clouds, they have cracked the code.

Years of experience, when left unexamined, is just the *illusion of competence wearing aftershave.* Do not be fooled by the corporate veteran who says, "I have done this for 30 years." That is not a badge of mastery, but, more simply, a sign that they have managed to avoid being fired. What matters is not the *duration of experience,* but the *depth* of it. The number of years means nothing if those years were not marked by real learning, reflection, and being proven wrong. In fact, the longer someone has done something without being challenged or exposed to real feedback, the more skeptical you should be.

The more stories you hear of miracle rainmakers, the more you should check the forecast, because if you are betting your business on them, you might just be worshipping a dancer.

This reminds me of Matthias, an old colleague: German to the bone, sharp as a shard of glass, and as precise as a Swiss watch (but don't tell him I compare him to anything Swiss). Matthias used to literally run half-marathons before breakfast, not for fun, but because his body demanded it the way other people crave coffee. He would attend meetings fresh from a 10 Km run, barely breaking a sweat, while the rest of us were still nursing our third cup of espresso. For all his German precision, though, his one great indulgence was Thai food, specifically the spiciest dishes imaginable. While most of us would cautiously poke at a plate of

Pad Thai, Matthias would be gleefully demolishing a bowl of something so fiery it could melt a hole through the table. He would take a bite, pause for a moment as if running an internal systems check, and then nod approvingly: "Ah, yes. Just the right amount of pain." That was Matthias in a nutshell: brilliant, disciplined, slightly terrifying, and utterly unfazed by things that would leave most people in tears.

Matthias had a catchy way to describe the futility of experience:

> "I don't care how many years of experience you have. You can do things wrong for a lifetime."

Build your Circle of Critics

Not all criticism is constructive, of course. Distinguishing between what is useful and what is merely demoralizing is a skill in itself.

Everyone needs a *Circle of Critics*, a personal *Knights of the Round Table* of trusted colleagues, mentors, and even family members who you find reliable to give honest and constructive feedback. These are the people whose opinions are laced with the intention of aiding your growth and not just pointing out your shortcomings.

A trusted circle of people who care about you and don't look at each interaction with you as a transactional exchange is amongst the most powerful tactics you can use to elevate yourself.

I still do it.

My favorite is a group chat on Signal with a bunch of friends that I highly respect and with whom I share elements of my professional background, life values, interests, and sense of humor. It is a beautiful mix of profound insights, terrible memes, and wildly inappropriate jokes that could get all of us canceled if leaked. At any given moment, the conversation can swing from a serious discussion on macroeconomic trends to someone dropping a photo of their disastrous attempt at homemade pizza. One minute, we are debating AI's impact on consulting, and the next, someone is sending a voice note of themselves ranting about airline lounge food like it is a UN crisis. The best part is that no one in this chat has any patience for nonsense. If someone posts an overly polished, LinkedIn-style *thought leadership* take, they get roasted instantly. Typos are ruthlessly mocked. If someone disappears for a few days, they return to find at least 847 unread messages, half of which are inside jokes they no longer understand. I love this type of mess because, on balance, it pushes me forward.

Think hard about who to let into your circle of critics. If it's true that we become the average of the five people we spend most of our time with, your critics will shape your thinking and behaviors prominently.

Oscar Wilde was almost entirely correct when he said: "Experience is simply the name we give our mistakes." In consulting, where delivery timelines are always tight, you don't have the luxury of unlimited time to learn only from your own experiences. Therefore, when leveraged effectively, criticism can supercharge your learning curve and make it faster.

Next time you find your temperature rising due to a critique about your precious report or slide deck, take a deep breath and be grateful that someone cares enough to point out the blind spots in your skillset. If you have a trusted Circle of Critics, you can easily evaluate the usability of the feedback and get to work on being the best damn consultant you can be.

Because, at the end of the day, criticism is nothing but love in work clothes, given with the goal to improve you. This is not a *feel-good mantra* (I hate those as much as you do) but a harsh reality.

Time is a scarce commodity. When someone, especially in a high-paced, performance-driven industry such as consulting, takes the time to point out your areas of improvement, it means that they see potential in you. Why would they invest the effort to dissect your work, identify your weaknesses, and share your thoughts?

Let me tell you why.

When I joined Accenture in Italy, part of the induction process involved meeting a Partner from the organization, one of those seasoned, slightly intimidating figures who had seen enough junior consultants come and go to know that most of us would be useless for at least a year. In his speech, he encouraged us to view the job as a long-term learning tool, and I now realize that building a career is a journey that spans decades, not something that happens in just a few months.

During that discussion, he instructed us to ask questions all the time, assuring us that our managers would always make time.

Now, I was young, but not naïve. Why would these busy, overworked people, drowning in deadlines and client demands, drop everything to answer my rookie-level questions? Charity? Altruism? A deep love for nurturing young talent?

Of course not. He explained how they had a vested interest. This is the fundamental reality of corporate mentorship: they teach you not out of kindness (although, sometimes, that too can happen) but because ignorance is expensive. Your incompetence is their liability. Your bosses are investing in an *asset* (that's you!) that will help them achieve their goals more efficiently. And since they have been around far longer than you have, they are more likely to spot the red flags you might be oblivious to.

The trick is to embrace this dynamic. Learn fast. Absorb everything. Become the consultant who does not just reduce your manager's headaches but actively helps them win. Because when you transition from being an *asset in training* to an *asset in motion*, that is the moment when you rise. That is the moment when you stop being a cost and start being invaluable.

Choose your mentors wisely. The competitive pie-eating contest in the professional services world can be isolating, as it can lead to a feeling of being emotionally ravaged, equivalent to being deserted in a ghost town. Having someone offer polite critique or share a laugh is an underrated necessity for a sustained career.

Learn from mentors how to operate, and from anti-mentors how not to operate.

What is an anti-mentor? I will tell you in the next chapter.

***

Vignette

Morrie is at his desk, trying to catch-up on his 43 unread emails after a 2-hour workshop with a client. Ivy storms in, dropping a deck of slides with a dramatic thud.

Ivy: Jacob torched my deck. In front of everyone. It was a public execution. I am *this close* to just moving to Bali and selling smoothies.
Morrie [glancing up from his pencil, unimpressed]: And what would you call the smoothie stand? "Pity & Pineapple"?
Ivy [glowering]: This is serious! He tore my work apart like... like...
Morrie: Like a consultant being paid to make you better?
Ivy [gritting teeth]: Still hurt.
Morrie: Of course it hurt. You are not a robot. You got your tuition served. You paid in bruised ego, and got clarity in return.
Ivy [sullen]: Feels like I got mugged.
Morrie [smirking]: Only because you tried to pay with Monopoly money. Come back with real ideas next time. And maybe... maybe keep a tiny bit less of your self-worth in a PowerPoint file.

***

Practical exercises

To practice the key ideas discussed in this chapter, work on the following three actionable exercises:

Daily self-reflection
Activity: Set aside 10 minutes at the end of each day for self-reflection. Find a quiet space and think about the feedback you received throughout the day, your reactions, and how your ego may have influenced those reactions. Jot down any insights or patterns you notice in a journal.
Objective: To build self-awareness, and recognize how ego impacts your response to criticism. Regularly reflecting will make you more mindful of your reactions and better prepared to handle feedback constructively.

Feedback seeking
Activity: In your next meeting or one-on-one with a mentor or colleague, actively seek performance feedback. Ask specific questions about areas you seek improvement, listen without interrupting or defending, and note the feedback. Express gratitude for the insights.
Objective: To normalize the process of receiving feedback and demonstrate radical openness. Seeking feedback regularly helps identify blind spots, and accelerates skill development.

The Three C's Technique
Activity: When you receive criticism, immediately apply the Three C's Technique.
1) Clarify: Ask questions to fully understand the feedback. Get examples if needed.

2) Consider: Reflect on the feedback objectively. Assess its validity without letting emotions cloud your judgment.
3) Choose: Decide on actionable steps to address the feedback. Make a plan and set a timeline for implementing these changes.
Objective: To provide a structured approach for processing criticism. By clarifying, considering, and choosing your response, you ensure that feedback is transformed into actionable insights, leading to tangible improvements in your work and personal growth.

Some mentors are warnings, not blueprints

Midway upon the journey of my consulting life, I found myself in a dark wood, not of existential dread, but of endless status meetings and inboxes bloated with "gentle reminders." Unlike Dante, who had Virgil to guide him through the *circles of hell*, I had no such luck.

For those of you who did not suffer through a classical education in Italy, Dante Alighieri was a 14th-century Italian poet, best known for writing *The Divine Comedy*, an epic three-part journey through Hell (*Inferno*), Purgatory (*Purgatorio*), and Heaven (*Paradiso*). It is arguably the most ambitious self-help book ever written, if you consider "not being eternally damned" to be good life advice. In *Inferno*, Dante is guided through Hell by the Roman poet Virgil, observing sinners trapped in their tailor-made punishments. The lustful are tossed around by violent winds (because they let their passions control them), the greedy are crushed under boulders of their own wealth, and traitors, such as Judas and Brutus, are eternally chewed on by Satan himself.

Subtlety was not Dante's strong suit.

Dante would not need to invent poetic punishments if he were alive today. He could just take a tour of the modern workplace: corporate life, like Hell, can have its own layers of torment.

There is the *Circle of the Spreadsheet Tyrants*, where obsessive managers believe that if something cannot be measured, it must not exist. If they had lived in the Renaissance, they would have requested Michelangelo to provide a weekly utilization report while painting the Sistine Chapel.

Then comes the *Circle of the Jargon Mongers*, where souls are damned to an eternity of *leveraging synergies* and *taking this offline*. Their punishment is poetic justice: forced to listen to their own words, on loop, in a never-ending strategy offsite.

Lower still is the *Circle of the Talent Butchers*, those charming executives who believe human capital is just another disposable asset, like toner cartridges. These are the types who *optimize headcount* (read: fire people) while giving keynote speeches on leadership. If Dante were writing today, he would place them right next to Judas and Brutus, except instead of betraying Caesar, they betray their teams for a slightly better operating margin.

And yet, dear reader, these people are not entirely useless, far from it.

If the good mentors show us what to do, these poor souls serve another, equally valuable function: they teach us, in painful detail, what to avoid at all costs. Learning from great leaders is terrific, but often impractical: you cannot just copy Marcus Aurelius and expect people to call you *wise*. However, spotting an incompetent buffoon in a meeting and vowing to never, ever behave like them is, actually, real practical education.

Let us begin.

Teachings from an anti-mentor

It was a sweltering afternoon, and I was sitting in a cramped office with Andrew, a senior leader renowned for saving failing businesses by fixing technology issues that nobody believed could be fixed. His track record was stellar, but sit with the guy for ten minutes and you realize, in no uncertain terms, that he is also a prime example of how *not* to become. Andrew was tall in the way those inflatable car dealership mascots are tall. Bald as a billiard ball, with a face so hairless it looked like it had been sanded, he had zero sense of humor. None. He once stared blankly at a joke I made about SAP migrations and finance workflows (a certified crowd-pleaser, in consultant circles), and then said, in all seriousness, "I do not understand. Procurement is not funny."

The real show began when he was concentrating. He would freeze, mouth ever so slightly ajar, eyes laser-locked on whatever diagram or spreadsheet was in front of him. The expression made him look like he had just walked into a room and forgotten why, or like he was trying to remember the name of his childhood dentist. He also liked to eat apples, religiously, one per afternoon. Watching him doing it was a pain: it took him so long. He would bite, chew, stare into the void like he was solving *Fermat's Last Theorem*, then, five minutes later, bite again. I once timed him: an hour and twenty-six minutes, for one apple. I am fairly sure he thought digestion was a form of risk management. It was a kind of dumbfounded genius, if that makes any sense. Andrew was someone who could design an entire banking integration architecture but might accidentally microwave a fork.

He spoke with a deep, deliberate voice, and moved like he was operating on a different frame rate: always slow, mechanical, precise. His leadership style was the managerial equivalent of blunt-force trauma. Andrew was an *anti-mentor*, someone whose sole contribution to your growth is showing you, with mathematical precision, what not to do.

Some mentors teach by example. Andrew taught by counterexample.

Don't get me wrong, Andrew was a genius when dealing with APIs and systems architecture. He could glance at a table and tell you where the inefficiencies lay and how to improve poor metrics. He knew so much about finance that I could always learn something new just by sitting next to him: breathing the same oxygen was an educational experience.

However, his emotional intelligence was absolutely null.

Forget work-life balance. He would regularly call you on your day off for a non-urgent matter, a *quick question* which would turn into a 90-minute interrogation. Andrew was all about results and gave zero fucks to the human element.

We were collaborating on a massive project integrating a client's legacy accounting system into a new ERP. The stakes were sky-high, with millions of dollars in potential cost savings on the line. Andrew was laser-focused on efficiencies and OKRs, but something else was also evident: he was utterly tone-deaf to the emotional climate of his team.

Case in point: Richard, one of our most diligent junior consultants, was visibly struggling with the new software interface.

For anyone else, this would be a big sign flashing "Needs Support!" but Andrew's response was, let's say, *different*. In a team meeting, he delivered his verdict with all the warmth of an industrial meat processor: "Let's not forget we are not here for a learning curve. If you can't keep up, maybe you are in the wrong room."

Boom! The tension was palpable. This is the moment where an organization loses people: not physically, not immediately, but mentally. It is the precise leadership style that makes talented professionals start updating their résumés before lunch.

Any reasonable leader would have pulled Richard aside, given him targeted coaching, or offered additional training sessions. Any reasonable leader, but not Andrew. He just wanted to up the "efficiency" metrics, regardless of the human toll.

This was not just a one-off event.

Andrew had a knack for turning simple conversations into torture chambers. A one-on-one meeting with him felt like you were a line item on a balance sheet: necessary, yet utterly devoid of value beyond your ability to contribute to the bottom line.

He would ask about your weekend only to transition into: "Good, good, now about that functional specification..." as though human interaction was a minor inconvenience on his critical path.

You might think: "Well, the guy is successful, right? What's the issue?"

Hold up.

The thing with Andrew was that he had a revolving door of employees on his team. Talented people came, saw the madness, and often ran for the hills. I stuck around longer, not because I wanted to emulate him, but because I realized the value of understanding what not to do.

It is one thing to learn how to steer the ship; it is another to know what icebergs to avoid.

During my time with Andrew, I watched him micromanage to the point of absurdity.

Delegation was a foreign concept to him. He drowned in minutiae, burned through his team, and operated under the delusion that only he could get things done right. This is the paradox of the hyper-efficient manager: in the pursuit of control, they create inefficiency. I observed this, made mental notes, and promised myself that when I got to a position of leadership, I would trust my team.

Learning to delegate or respect personal boundaries is not the most important thing I learned from my infamous anti-mentor.

Watching Andrew in action taught me the importance of empathy in leadership. I witnessed client meetings where his lack of emotional intelligence killed potential deals. He was a bull in a china shop, charging through delicate negotiations with the finesse of a wrecking ball. Andrew had some business acumen but completely missed the *soft* skills that often make or break a deal.

That's why he became my anti-mentor: a walking and talking case study in what not to do.

How to convert observations into actionable insights

When you are just starting your business career, you find yourself in a unique vantage point from which you can see different leadership styles, work ethics, and project management approaches up close without any external burden of office politics or responsibilities. I'll tell you a story.

Let's say you are an intern and get staffed on a project with Ana, a former colleague of mine and a mid-level consultant notorious for her poor communication skills. Your gut reaction might be: "Damn, why did I get stuck with her?"

I urge you to think differently.

Instead of dreading the experience, see it as a live case study on how not to be. Ana becomes your anti-mentor for communication. Observe how her lack of clarity impacts the team's morale, the project's progress, and even the client's faith in your firm. Take mental notes: How could this situation be improved? How would you handle it differently?

Let me tell you more about Ana, because once you meet her, you will not forget her. Born in the former Yugoslavia, Ana had the no-nonsense air of someone who had seen tougher things in life than a delayed PowerPoint deck. She had the presence of a Soviet-era tank commander, built like a small but unshakable fortress, with broad shoulders, sharp cheekbones, and an expression that could make junior consultants rethink their entire career choices. She wore structured blazers in dark colors, as if dressing for a battle that only she could see coming, and she moved with the efficiency of a person who had no time for pleasantries or, frankly, for you.

I always thought her emails were a masterclass in ambiguity. A three-word response from Ana could mean anything from "Good job" to "Fix everything immediately, you idiot". If you asked her to clarify, she would look at you like you had just failed the most basic test of intelligence. In meetings, she spoke in abrupt thoughts, often assuming that everyone could read between lines that did not even exist. Yet, despite her terrifying presence, Ana was a true domain expert. The problem was that she assumed everyone else was operating at her level, which, as reality has repeatedly shown, is never the case.

One of the best moments of Ana-lore happened in a client meeting. She asked a junior consultant a fairly standard question about the project. The poor guy, fresh-faced and hopeful, responded with the worst possible phrase:

"Let me check because I don't remember."

Silence.

Ana stared at him as if he had just confessed to a federal crime, and then, with the casual venom of a person who has no time for mediocrity, said:

"If you ask me about my work, I will always have an answer. Wake me up at 3 am, drunk, half-conscious, I will still give you every detail without missing a beat."

The junior consultant (who, to be clear, was not managing the national debt of a collapsing economy) nodded solemnly, as if he had just been granted access to an ancient guild where total recall was the only acceptable form of competence. From that day forward, the kid always had an answer. Whether awake, half-asleep, or possibly even in a coma, he was ready, just in case Ana ever decided to test him at 3 am with a bottle of home-made rakija in hand.

That is where your opportunity lies. Learn from Ana, not in the way she would have intended, but in the way that will serve you best. If she is the worst communicator in the room, make sure you become the best.

Fast-forward a few months, or maybe even years: you are now leading a smaller project and must deliver some complex information to your team.

Cue a flashback to Ana.

You remember how her vague emails led to that mini-crisis around deliverable deadlines. So, what do you do?

You take the anti-Ana approach: a clearly laid out email, bullet points and all, followed by a quick huddle to ensure everyone is on the same page.

Et voila, you have just sidestepped a potential pitfall by learning from your anti-mentor.

Another quick example.

Have you ever worked under a manager who is all about utilization rates but cannot care less about the human element? I have. It sucks.

Your immediate takeaway should be: *When I'm in a managerial role, I'll make sure to check in on my team's well-being, not just their billable hours.* It's that simple. Your anti-mentor has just taught you a valuable lesson in leadership and human resource management without even knowing it.

Learning from an anti-mentor does not mean actively seeking out poor examples; you must adapt your behaviors based on positive and negative examples around you.

Whenever I found myself in tricky situations, I asked myself: *What would Andrew do?* And then, quite consciously, I would do the opposite.

This is a textbook example of *via negativa*, a term used to describe knowledge or wisdom gained through elimination, i.e., understanding what not to do.

Every time Andrew fails to show empathy, he unknowingly provides a lesson in the importance of emotional intelligence in the workplace. He is a cautionary tale, an object lesson in how not to manage a team or run a project.

It's not all bad

Your good experiences will hopefully outnumber the bad ones throughout a long career. I know that's how it worked out for me.

The vast majority of leaders I was associated with over the last two decades were great mentors for me. Ron, a British Program Director I was lucky enough to work for during my semi-senior years, is the best example of an empathetic, kind leader who always did everything he could to put his team at ease. And by "put his team at ease", I mean he had the emotional intelligence of a therapist and the mouth of a 1980s pub regular who had just lost a bet.

Ron was a red-faced bloke with a perpetually mischievous grin, like he had just thought of an inappropriate joke but was deciding whether HR would let him get away with it. He had the build of a man who had never once skipped a full English breakfast and the energy of someone who drank his tea strong enough to dissolve metal. On his upper right arm, barely hidden under *industrial-strength* cotton shirts, was a large barcode tattoo, a relic from a wilder decade, and a daily reminder that some branding is harder to undo than others. His accent was thick, Midlands-born but sprinkled with Cockney rhyming slang, a linguistic disaster for anyone not raised in a London market stall (imagine for a young Italian guy who could barely speak common English!).

One day, he told me to "use me loaf." I stared at him, confused. He sighed and explained, "Loaf of bread. Head. Use your bloody head, mate." That was lesson one. Lesson two came when he described a senior executive as "brown bread." Dead. The man was very much alive but, according to Ron, his career was already in the grave. Ron was not always politically correct, but he was never mean-spirited. His humor came from a place of warmth, and even when he called someone a "right plonker," it somehow felt like a term of endearment.

He believed in his people and had a way of making you feel like a million bucks while simultaneously roasting you for whatever mistake you had just made. If you delivered a good piece of work, Ron would say: "Well done, son. Almost like you know what you're doing." If you messed up, he would shake his head, sigh dramatically, and say: "That was a dog's breakfast, but we'll fix it before the muppets upstairs notice." And yet, for all his wisecracks, Ron was the guy you wanted in your corner. He fought for his team, took bullets for them when things went south, and somehow made the most stressful projects feel like an inside joke.

By the time I stopped working with Ron, I had learned three things: how to run a complex program, how to survive corporate nonsense with humor, and enough Cockney rhyming slang to confuse every taxi driver I have ever met.

I remember, on one occasion, I had to send a bad email to a senior client to explain an issue that had been caused by a mistake by a team member. This was really making me nervous.

This was a demanding client.

Ron suggested I draft the email with as many details as possible (I was much closer to the groundwork than him). He would then add what he called "a bit of Ron's magic" to make the communication more palatable.

Clearly, he was trying his best to safeguard me and the team while delivering accurate information to the client without adding more pressure on me or the other guys because of the mistakes that had caused that specific problem.

I liked that approach because, as strange as it might sound, it was the first time in my career that my boss got into the trenches at that level of detail not to micromanage, not to assert dominance, but to help.

It could seem like nothing special to an outsider. "So what? He helped tweak an email." In the real world, where corporate leaders are often too busy crafting manifestos on 'collaboration' while leaving their teams to fend for themselves, this was a revelation. People do not need grand speeches or LinkedIn-friendly mission statements. They need cover fire when it matters.

These days, when I see one of my team members hesitating before sending a tough email, I know what is happening. The invisible anxiety, the pressure, the fear of phrasing something the wrong way and setting off a nuclear chain reaction. I recognize it because I have been there. And so, I do what Ron did. I step in. I work with them, not as a superior, but as someone who has been in the exact same foxhole. We fix it together.

We all screw up. We all get things wrong. The difference between a strong team and a dysfunctional one is simple: how mistakes are handled. Do you let people drown, or do you throw them a rope? Do you act like Andrew, blaming and belittling, or do you act like Ron, shielding and guiding? In your early years, you will find yourself surrounded by all kinds of professionals: some who inspire, some who drain the life out of the room, and some who teach you, unintentionally, how not to be. Anti-mentors like Andrew and Ana are helpful, but only if you extract the lesson: "That? Never doing that."

Rejecting the bad is only half the equation.

What will you do? How will you lead? And what will you measure?

Let's keep moving, pal, to find out what else happens in consulting beyond slides. We are just halfway there.

***

Vignette

Morrie and Ivy are hanging out in Morrie's office. Ivy keeps glancing at a battered old folder stuffed with messy papers. Unable to resist, he grabs it and reads the label out loud.

Ivy: "Anti-Mentors and Epic Fails"? What the hell is this?
Morrie [grinning]: The best lessons I ever learned… from the worst people I ever worked with. Sometimes, the best teacher is a bad example.
Ivy [wide-eyed]: This is like consulting's villain handbook.
Morrie: You would not be wrong. A bad consultant is basically a slow-burning supervillain… For the client *and* the team.
Ivy [flipping through pages]: "Micromanagement Meltdown"… "Communication Catastrophe"… "Apathetic Assassins"… These sound like rejected comic book villains.
Morrie: They are cautionary tales. Villains exist to remind you what not to become.
Ivy [grinning]: Got it. Learn from the villains, become the superhero consultant. Where is my cape?
Morrie [deadpan]: Nah. skip the cape. You will trip over it. Stick to a good suit… or a black shirt and shorts. [smirking] Just remember to frame the camera right when you work from home: people don't want to see your naked legs.

***

Practical exercises

To practice the key ideas discussed in this chapter, work on the following three actionable exercises:

The anti-mentor reflection

Activity: Think of a time you encountered an "anti-mentor" like Andrew in your career. Write a short reflection about this interaction, focusing on the negative behaviors you observed, and how they impacted you and those around you.

Objective: This exercise aims to enhance self-awareness and critical thinking by reflecting on negative examples in your professional environment, helping you identify what leadership behaviors to avoid.

The positive flip

Activity: Take the negative behaviors you have identified in your anti-mentor and write down how you would approach these situations differently. For instance, if your anti-mentor lacked empathy in client meetings, outline how you would demonstrate empathy in a similar scenario.

Objective: The goal here is to transform negative observations into positive actions you can take in your career, reinforcing learning from adverse examples by actively planning to do the opposite.

Role-play the right way

Activity: Pair up with a colleague or friend, and role-play a scenario where you are in a leadership position similar to your anti-mentor's. Your partner will act as a team member facing an issue. Practice responding in a way that counteracts your anti-mentor's approach, focusing on positive leadership behaviors.

Objective: This exercise is designed to put theory into practice by simulating real-life situations where you can apply the positive flips you have identified, enhancing your soft skills in leadership and communication.

ONLY FOOLS BLINDLY OBEY RULES THEY DID NOT WRITE

Let me tell you a story about Julius Caesar, not yet the battlefield-conquering, empire-building legend most people remember, but the young 25-year-old still practically unknown Roman with little more than ambition and guts.

Back in 75 BC, Caesar was captured by Cilician pirates while crossing the Aegean Sea. The pirates, not particularly bright, demanded a ransom of *20 talents* of silver. Caesar, with the audacity of someone who thought destiny owed him a throne, laughed at them, insisting he was worth at least *50 talents*. Not only that, but he also promised to hunt them down and crucify them once he was free (you know, as one does). The pirates, amused and possibly thinking Caesar was just another rich, spoiled Roman, let him send his friends to gather the ransom. While waiting for the money, Caesar acted not like a prisoner but like a leader: he demanded respect from his captors, made them listen to his speeches, recited poetry to them, even joined them in their games. He was performing, yes, but also building his own system of influence in enemy territory. By the time the ransom was paid and he was released, 38 days later, the pirates probably thought they had made a friend.

Caesar, of course, was not joking about his threat. He immediately raised a fleet, hunted down the pirates, and crucified the lot of them. Actually, he made sure to cut their throats first, which was a gesture of mercy by Roman standards: Julius Caesar was a nice guy after all.

The lesson here is in understanding that Caesar did not just react to his situation but completely redefined it. He did not play by the rules of captivity. He reshaped his environment, turning his imprisonment into a stage where *he* was the one commanding respect and dictating the terms. Once free, he doubled down, proving that he was worth far more than his captors ever imagined.

Here's why this matters to you: in the corporate world, particularly in consulting, the rules and metrics you are given, the *standard KPIs,* are often just another form of captivity. They measure what is easy to count, not what truly counts. Utilization rates, billable hours, client satisfaction scores, are the minimum requirements to stay in the game, not the pathway to greatness.

If you accept those metrics as the final word, you are no different from Caesar's pirates, thinking small, thinking conventionally. Suppose you redefine what success looks like and build your framework of performance metrics that highlight your unique contributions and value. In that case, you are *rewriting the game rules to win* (shoutout to Roger L. Martin). Like Caesar, when you eventually deliver the goods, everyone will realize you were worth far more than they ever expected.

My question to you is: are you ready to create your own metrics, ones that showcase your actual value, not just your compliance with someone else's definition of success?

You walk into your new consulting job all bright-eyed and bushy-tailed. During your orientation session, you are handed a job description that is denser than a brick, which mentions metrics you have never heard before.

The words barely mean anything to you yet, but you are told these KPIs will define the longevity of your career. It feels like you have been given the primal keys of corporate validation, and you start chasing those parameters like a greyhound after a rabbit. It is easy to get sucked into thinking that these metrics are the be-all and end-all of your consulting career. I call such ringing thoughts the *Illusion of Completeness.*

You start to believe you are set if you nail these numbers, but that's like confusing the forest for the trees. It is essential to realize that these KPIs only tell part of the story, especially for younger consultants who are still learning the ropes. These metrics do not measure how adaptable you are, how innovative you can be, or even how empathetic you behave with your clients and teammates.

What should you do then?

First, don't throw these traditional KPIs out the window.

Traditional KPIs

Let's get one thing straight: traditional KPIs are the bread and butter of consulting. Ignore them, and you might as well pack your bags and start a goat cheese farm in the Alps. We are talking about the classics here: utilization rate (a.k.a. how much of your life belongs to the client), client satisfaction scores (a.k.a. proof you did not completely botch the job), and all the other pretty little metrics that make Partners sleep soundly at night.

They matter because they are directly wired to the bottom line, the supreme green of dollars. Utilization rates, for instance, give a neat little snapshot of how well you are being *utilized* to generate revenue. High utilization makes you look like a golden goose in Partners' meetings, which means they will fight to have you on their projects. It is a beautiful little cycle: be in demand, get high utilization; have high utilization, stay in demand. Sure, it is simplistic, but that is corporate math for you.

Do not make the rookie mistake of scoffing at these metrics. These KPIs are non negotiable. They are the cost of entry, the table stakes that keep you in the game. Nail them, respect them, but understand that, while they will make you look good on paper, they will never make you a legendary consultant.

Supplement them with other metrics that capture your unique value.

You may be the go-to person for turning client presentations around in record time or have an eagle eye for operational inefficiencies that everyone else misses. These skills might be challenging to quantify, but they act as catalysts. These KPIs do not affect the bottom line directly, but they compound your career growth in the long run: they make you the person who gets remembered when the stakes are high.

The idea is to create a portfolio of KPIs tailored to you.

Tailor-made KPIs

Let's get real for a second. You are reading this because you want to stand out. If you want to stand out, then you have to ditch the idea that your value can be neatly summarized by whatever factory-grade KPIs your firm shoves in your direction.

If you want to rise above the noise, you need to create your own metrics. Call them *Tailor-made KPIs*. Call them *Personal Benchmarks of Awesomeness*. Call them whatever you want. The point is: you design the game, you define the rules, and, suddenly, you are the only one playing.

Let me give you 3 steps to follow.

Step 1: The art of sniffing out your value

Here's how you do it.

- Consult your mentors: Make your 'Circle of Critics' your first pitstop. Discuss your ambitions, and request their take on what parameters might be good indicators of your unique strengths. They might also share how they have measured their success beyond the conventional corporate metrics. You want radically honest feedback to help you identify strengths you did not even know you had. They might tell you that your "unique ability to empathize with clients" is about as valuable as a refrigerator in Antarctica. Or they will tell you it is gold, and you'd better start refining it. Whatever it is, it should be accurate.

- Talk to your peers: It's not just about vertical relationships; horizontal ones matter, too. Your colleagues are in the trenches with you and can offer perspectives on what additional skills or attributes could set you apart. Yes, your colleagues are *technically* your competition, but they are also your intelligence network. Pay attention to what they notice about you, especially the skills and attributes they find difficult to replicate. Find the gaps you fill better than anyone else, and make those gaps your personal property.

- Client feedback loop: With time, create a system for receiving informal client feedback. A casual chat after a project completion can offer invaluable information. In these scenarios, you are looking for what made you stand out in their eyes. Was it your problem-solving ability? Your knack for making complex issues digestible? Your communication skills à la Steve Jobs?

What you want is off-the-record commentary. Listen carefully, because clients will often reveal what actually impressed them, rather than what your firm *wanted* them to be impressed by.

- Shadow different roles: Spend some time shadowing people in various roles within your project. You will be amazed at how a different lens can inform you about metrics that matter but are rarely talked about. For example, working closely with your Project Manager, you may realize that risk mitigation is a fundamental component of running the project, but it is also vital when dealing with other adjacent specific activities. Not many consultants naturally think of ways to mitigate issues in their day-to-day lives, but you do, and should exploit this trait as a strength. Or, even as an early-career consultant, you have many contacts in the industry that could turn into business for your firm. Working closely with your Directors or Partners, you figure out that this is part of the assets you bring to your organization, even if not formally as part of your KPIs.

Step 2: Cataloging the invisible

Alright, so now you have an idea of your unique strengths. But let's be clear: if it is not written down, it does not exist. Your bosses are not mind readers (you are lucky if they remember your name after a busy week). So here's what you do:

- Capture the unquantifiable: These metrics are not generally measured but are invaluable. Did you resolve a team conflict that was hindering project performance? Did you streamline a work process that cut down task completion time? These things matter, and should be part of your personal performance narrative. You may believe your manager will notice that stuff anyway, but don't forget your career is your business: it is in your interest to remind them of what you have achieved, especially for those things that are not easily quantifiable. Keep a *brag file*: a spreadsheet or a couple of slides is sufficient. Every time you hit one of these custom KPIs, note the date and jot a comment. If a client sends you an email praising your hard work and excellent output, keep track of it. Log it. If you win an award at the organization you are currently deployed to, don't forget about it.

- Translate into actionable goals: Time to be creative. Let's say you have identified *conflict resolution* as a soft skill you excel at. Now, turn that into an actionable metric. How many conflicts did you successfully mediate? Did the project performance improve as a result? Mention that. Or, let's imagine that you are great at building relationships and, while working on a project, you managed to establish a good rapport with a businessperson who owns a significant budget. You introduced your friend to your boss, and, a few weeks later, a new project was sold. What revenue was directly linked to your introduction? Track it.

Step 3: Bring it all together and move up the ladder

Documentation is the prerequisite. Here comes the fun part: shoving your brilliance in front of the people who matter.

- Frame it right: When you present your *Tailor-made KPIs* to your boss, it is not a humblebrag but a presentation of facts. "Dear boss, I am not just meeting the baseline KPIs but I am also producing value in areas A, B, and C, which nobody else is even thinking about. Here's the proof." It works like magic: even if they are skeptical, you have now planted a seed in their minds that you are not just a worker bee. You are a creator of value.

- Break the comparison game: You want to stand out. You want to be *seen* and *felt* as different. You want to be entirely focused on your strengths. Your objective is to make yourself incomparable (if they can compare you to somebody else, that somebody else can, one day, also replace you). You must build a reputation around unique contributions that nobody else in your team, practice, or firm offers. When you become the person who handles the elusive 10% of work nobody else can touch, you stop being just another consultant whining about missed promotions. You will not be the guy griping to his mom, ranting to his barber, awkwardly hinting to his boss, and worst of all, unloading his frustration on his unsuspecting spouse.

Sometimes, the most impactful plays don't appear on the stats sheet.

Let me tell you about Rose.

She was a junior consultant in her late 20s, assigned to work with me on a major process optimization project for a large bank. On paper, she ticked every box: top graduate from one of the sandstone universities, black hair tied in a no-nonsense bun, the quiet confidence that comes from years of being pushed to do better, by family, by school, by herself. Rose was of Asian descent, first generation, raised in a home where education was not optional, and *do your best* meant *be the best*. But she had something else too. You could see it in her posture: upright, alert. You could see it in her habits. She woke up early to run, trained with a personal trainer on weekends, played tennis like she was chasing a grand slam. She once told me, almost apologetically, that weightlifting had helped her manage stress better than any mindfulness app ever could.

What made Rose stand out was not *just* her work ethic or her polished deliverables. It was the way she tuned into the emotional undercurrents in the room. While others focused on the workflows, the handoffs, the systems, she paid attention to the people in them. Rose was fascinated by the human element of consulting. Specifically, she was interested in employee engagement and how it affected productivity.

She knew that traditional metrics like utilization rates and billable hours would be key in her performance review. However, she also understood that this client engagement offered her a unique opportunity to flex a few additional muscles.

For the first few weeks, Rose played the part. She churned out models, ran numbers, and attended all the mind-numbingly long status update meetings. She was hitting all the standard KPIs out of the park. But she also started conducting mini one-on-one interviews with some of the bank's middle managers and rank-and-file employees, trying to get a handle on the organization's pulse.

She used these insights to add layers to her Excel models. She included metrics that factored in employee sentiment, departmental communication breakdowns, and other *soft* elements. Our project manager was initially skeptical, but when they started to see correlations between these factors and productivity, well, let's just say Rose got a lot more than a pat on the back.

During the project's closing presentation, Rose had her section where she got to present these findings.

To say that the client's senior stakeholders were impressed would be an understatement: they had not expected this depth of insight from a process optimization project. One of the VPs even remarked: "These insights might just be what we didn't know we were looking for."

Post-project, not only did Rose get the highest rating on her team, but her additional metrics were discussed at several Partner meetings as an example of innovative client service. She started to build a brand around her. Rose received an accelerated promotion and was asked to lead an internal team, incorporating these "human element" metrics into future client engagements.

Rose did not disregard traditional KPIs; she simply did not limit herself to them. And by doing that, she managed to excel at her job AND carve out a unique niche for herself.

Another time, I used to work with Keith, who was my project lead for a discovery phase in the technology department of a large enterprise. He was a good guy, with phenomenal attention to detail and strong domain knowledge. I didn't ask him for anything more than running the project to exceptional execution, keeping the client happy while we could deliver the insights and recommendations we had committed to.

He did a great job at all that, but he also formed a very close bond with his business-side counterpart. That person introduced Keith to various colleagues, and before we knew it, we had a couple of other opportunities in the making.

Because Keith was doing a good job on his project and because he was able to forge a strong rapport with many client stakeholders, other people working for the organization were willing to work with him. This eventually led to a new project being sold for our firm, which reflected well in Keith's performance appraisal. He was naturally acting in a more senior position than his job title would require, which is what you want to see in people asking for a promotion.

Reminder: Not everything that can be counted counts, and not everything that counts can be counted.

The metrics you design for yourself should reflect your strengths, not just what the firm says is important. When you expand your vision to include these additional metrics, people start seeing you in a different light. You are not just doing a good job: you are redefining what a good job even means.

Surely, you are thinking: I haven't got time to do my standard job. How can I possibly do the extra bits? Well, read on: the next chapter should help you.

***

Vignette

Morrie and Ivy are in a meeting room with graphs and charts being projected on the wall. Ivy is visibly frustrated, while Morrie has a sly smile on his face.

Ivy: Morrie, these traditional KPIs are driving me nuts! Utilization rates, client satisfaction scores... I feel like I'm trapped in a numeric maze.
Morrie: Professional services adaptation of the Kafkaesque, don't you think?
Ivy: Not funny at all. It's my second project. I need to do more.
Morrie: But you have already —
Ivy: Ya ya, I know. I am improving, and it takes time ya da ya da. But I want to be different and better, you know. Go a little beyond.
Morrie [hands Ivy a colorful notebook labeled "Brag File" with doodles and stars]: When I was young and had a head full of hair, I used this to document my soft skills and unique approaches.
Ivy: Like your own tailor-made KPIs?
Morrie: Exactly! When you capture and showcase your unique value, you are memorable. Remember, the best moves often don't make the stat sheet.
Ivy: What is consulting if not an exercise in painfully aware narcissism?

***

Practical exercises

To practice the key ideas discussed in this chapter, work on the following three actionable exercises:

KPI reflection and expansion

Activity: Reflect on the traditional KPIs mentioned in your role and jot them down. Next to each, write a unique or 'soft' skill you possess that these KPIs do not capture but that contributes to your success and the team's.

Objective: This exercise aims to help you recognize the value you bring beyond standard metrics, encouraging you to think about your broader contributions to the team and projects.

Mentor consultation

Activity: Schedule a meeting with your mentor or a senior colleague you respect. Discuss the KPIs you have listed and the unique skills you have identified. Ask for their advice on quantifying or demonstrating these skills in your work.

Objective: The goal is to gain insight into how experienced professionals value and showcase skills that are not easily quantified, helping you to frame your unique contributions in a way that resonates with leadership.

Custom KPI development

Activity: Based on your reflection and mentor consultation, develop at least one custom KPI that captures your unique strength or contribution. For example, if you are great at resolving team conflicts, your KPI could be the number of conflicts resolved and the positive outcomes achieved.

Objective: This exercise encourages you to think creatively about measuring your contributions, preparing you to articulate and demonstrate your full value to the team and leadership beyond traditional metrics.

Sculpt Your Time Like a Surgeon and Guard It Like a Fortress

The first time I pulled an 80-hour week, I came really close to losing my mind.

You know how it goes. You are slogging away on a due diligence project for some megabank, and the client is breathing down your neck. The metrics your output is evaluated on don't care if you are sacrificing sleep, your social life, or even a decent meal to achieve them. So you just mumble: *This is what I signed up for,* and embrace your fate.

The truth is that it does not have to be this way.

A lot of ill-glamorized 80-hour weeks are smoke and mirrors. Theater. Bad theater, like a high school Shakespeare production where half the cast forgot their lines. You think you are grinding, but what you are actually doing is *shuffling*, desperately jumping between tasks, responding to emails the moment they ping, filling your schedule with "urgent" meetings. You are a hamster on a wheel, breaking a sweat but not moving an inch.

Let me tell you about the time I realized I was wasting hours on meaningless work; it was during one of my early ERP implementation projects. My manager had asked for a detailed benchmark analysis on dozens of invoice factoring clients, so I spent hours perfecting a massive spreadsheet with every possible metric: revenue, employee headcount, product features, customer segments, and probably a dozen more. I felt like a productivity machine. Then, in the final review, my manager barely glanced at it and said: "This is great, but all I needed was a quick summary on the top three clients. Can you distill this into a one-pager?" That was my wake-up call. I had burned an entire day deep in Excel hell, but if I had asked the right questions upfront, I could have saved myself hours and delivered precisely what mattered. That is when I realized that not all work is created equal, and effort does not always equal impact.

Consulting is hustle (and, if you choose this career, you are some sort of adrenaline junkie anyway) however, hand to my heart, a chaotic hustle is a recipe for burnout. Hence, let's bring the 80-20 rule into the picture, also known as the Pareto Principle.

The 80/20 Principle: your scalpel

Richard Koch, the co-founder of L.E.K. Consulting, has written extensively about the 80/20 principle, pushing it beyond its original scope as an economic principle into the realm of productivity. In his book *The 80/20 Principle: The Secret to Achieving More with Less*, Richard quotes Italian economist Vilfredo Pareto arguing that "the 80/20 Principle enables a minority of causes, inputs, or effort usually to lead a majority of the results, outputs, or rewards": 80% of results come from 20% of effort.

In consulting, this simple framework is the scalpel you need to slice away the garbage. This is the tool that lets you cut through the noise and identify the work that actually matters (because most of the work you are doing does not matter, sorry to break it to you).

Here's a quick litmus test: ask yourself, *Is this task going to help elevate my standing with the client or within my firm?* If the answer is a resounding yes, that's your 20%. If it's a maybe, then you have just found another piece of the 80% that deserves the bin.

Early in my consulting career, I thought every client conversation required a polished deck. Every idea and every discussion, I believed, had me producing formatted slides, sleek graphics, and bulletproof messaging. It was drilled into me: "Come prepared. Look professional." One day, I realized how much unnecessary work that mindset created.

I was working in Italy with a bank's CIO on a core banking transformation. My team and I were preparing for a meeting to discuss the high-level approach to a specific issue he wanted to address, and we were deep into crafting a polished 20-slide deck with perfect fonts and no detail left untouched. It was going to take us a couple of full days.

Then I asked myself: *WTF... Do we actually need this?*

The goal of the meeting was not to impress, but simply to test whether our thinking was directionally correct. So, instead of spending hours perfecting a slide deck, I sketched the key ideas on a whiteboard. Just raw thinking. When we met, the conversation was sharper. The CIO was engaged, debating ideas rather than passively flipping through slides. We identified gaps immediately, things that would have been buried in a deck. Instead of spending 48 hours perfecting slides, we used that time to refine the actual approach.

That was the moment I internalized the 80/20 rule in consulting. Most of the time, the deck is not the value: the thinking is! And when you are in an early conversation, you do not need to over-invest in polish. You need clarity.

Now, think of how many meetings you are asked to attend every day. Are they required? The answer is a clear *no* for many of them. I'm not suggesting you become a dissident and start ditching important sessions with your boss or your clients, but you must start looking at these time-consuming situations through a different lens. If work can happen asynchronously, perhaps take the initiative and suggest a different way of working. Show (don't tell) how the team could, half of the time, achieve the same results by updating a simple centralized repository with all the information, filling out a webform, or perhaps sending a short message with an update in the group chat. I know it sounds crazy to you, but replacing calls or meetings with a Teams message is possible. I have seen it done, and done well. I have a colleague who unapologetically refuses to be a slave to real-time interruptions. If you try to call him on his phone, or pull him into an *impromptu* virtual meeting, he will ignore it. Then, seconds later, you will get a simple message:

"I am deep into something right now. Not available for a call. Just drop me a message, and I will get back to you when I can."

The first time this happened to me, I will admit, I was annoyed. My instinct was to think: *Come on, just pick up. It will only take a minute.* But then I realized how often *just a minute* turns into fifteen. How frequently do quick calls spiral into unnecessary discussions? Over time, I came to appreciate his approach because his boundaries forced me to be more intentional. Instead of defaulting to a call, I started summarizing my thoughts in a Teams message. More often than not, I realized I did not need an immediate answer. A response within an hour or two was more than enough.

Because he protected his focus, when he *did* respond, his answers were clearer and more thoughtful: no half-baked on-the-fly responses, but well-considered input that actually moved things forward.

If you think you *must* always be available, challenge that assumption. Try it for a day. Ignore non-urgent calls and force asynchronous communication. You will be amazed at how much more you get done.

In his book *The burnout society*, South-Korean philosopher Byung-Chul Han writes:

> "We owe the cultural achievements of humanity—which include philosophy—to deep, contemplative attention. Culture presumes an environment in which deep attention is possible. Increasingly, such immersive reflection is being displaced by an entirely different form of attention: hyperattention. A rash change of focus between different tasks, sources of information, and processes characterizes this scattered mode of awareness."

Hyperactivity, the constant state of switching focus between tasks, devices, and distractions, has slowly become the norm. The *information overload*, a modern *intellectual obesity* we are constantly warned about, is not a mere inconvenience but a form of psychological theft. The frenetic rush we embrace, including the rapid ping of notifications and the endless scrolling of newsfeeds, does not add to our lives but depletes them.

I argue that real wealth lies not in *doing more*, but in carving out the space to do less: focusing on what is truly important, and allowing light boredom to become the incubation for new ideas. To regain your time means to first accept that most of what you are rushing toward is probably irrelevant. Every moment spent chasing the fleeting and trivial steals from the time needed to think, create, and observe the world with clarity.

Do you really care about those shows on Netflix? Are you really interested in that influencer you follow on Instagram? Does spending hours at the shopping center buying shit you don't need add anything to your life?

You can apply the same modus operandi to your job life.

Time blocking and deep work: your fortress

Your Outlook calendar should not be just used for setting reminders for your next Teams meeting. As a young consultant, your most valuable asset is not (yet) your expertise or your network: it's your time.

In his vast collection of works, William Penn, the English 1600s writer and early Quaker, writes extensively about time: "Time is what we want most but what we use worst." He couldn't be more correct! In fact, this message should be plastered on the walls of every consulting office, from New York to Sydney, because most consultants treat time like cheap office coffee: available, replaceable, endlessly squandered.

This is where Time Blocking comes in. You need to build a fortress around your most valuable activities.

Begin by acknowledging the ebb and flow of your cognitive abilities throughout the day. If you are a morning person, allocate the first block of your day for heavy-lifting tasks: problem-solving, thinking, or working on important client presentations. On the flip side, if you are a night owl, do not fool yourself into scheduling deep analytical work at 8 am: my friend Brad from Chicago would say that this is how PowerPoint slides end up looking like ransom notes.

Time blocking is about synchronizing your circadian rhythm (your body clock over a 24-hour cycle) with your to-do list. You are making a mental commitment by assigning specific chunks of time to tasks. You are creating a psychological contract with yourself. Start small with detailed tasks that you want to accomplish, and dedicate a block of your time to that task. When you are starting out, make that task the smallest possible to still be confident you are actually going to tackle it. If you have never run before, don't decide you are going to do the London Marathon next week...

Once, one of my colleagues asked me how I was able to be so well-organized, produce all the outputs assigned to me, and still attend all the meetings I was supposed to participate in.

This is my explanation, and it is a simple one.

I am at my best in the early hours of the day, so that is when I schedule the most creative work I have to do. I am not able to function as effectively in the afternoons and evenings: naturally, that is when I take care of administrative tasks, or some of the more repetitive activities I am responsible for.

During the first large program of work that I had to lead autonomously, I used to block some time after lunch to go for a walk around the block on my own, weaving through the glass-and-steel canyons of Milan's business district. The area was a dense maze of tall office buildings with barely a patch of green in sight: just endless concrete, the occasional potted plant outside a coffee shop, and the faint scent of exhaust fumes lingering in the air.

As I walked, I would pass sleek boutiques with minimalist window displays, impatient Vespa riders weaving through traffic while *swearing*, and the ever-present gelato places, with their neon-lit counters stacked with pastel-colored mounds of *pistacchio* and *stracciatella*. The streets were alive with hurried conversations in clipped Italian (mostly *swearing*), the rhythmic clatter of coffee cups in outdoor bars and the distant honking of a taxi driver losing patience (and *swearing* creatively).

That walk was my ritual, my chance to escape the chaos, let my mind replay the last 24 hours, and carve out a clear path forward before diving back into the storm.

The fortress is real. Build it. Guard it. When you do, you unlock the power of *Deep Work,* that state where you produce your best thinking and actually get things done, which is the concept introduced by Professor Cal Newport (yeah, you must have read that book), where the intersection of time management and effective execution lies.

You will have clients who see every email as a five-alarm fire.

In 1954, during one of his speeches, Dwight D. Eisenhower, the 34th President of the United States and a five-star general during World War II, presented the idea that would later lead to the Eisenhower Matrix. He quoted an unnamed university president when he said:

> "I have two kinds of problems, the *urgent* and the *important.* The urgent are not important, and the important are never urgent."

Yes, most urgent things are not actually important.

While in Asia, I was working on a project that was not doing that great. Everything was *urgent,* and at some point, I started to get emails with subject lines prefixed with the words "TOP URGENT." The client had to necessarily add that tag; otherwise, you would have run the risk of confusing the TOP URGENT tasks with other banally URGENT ones. It was pure madness.

The only way to get any work done was to counsel my peers and senior leaders on how to prioritize the clients' requests by providing detailed reasoning and tackling the top 20% of the issues first. It turns out the client did not care about the rest of the 80%, nor were they required for our overall deliverables.

Allocate your time wisely, put out the real fires, and let the other ones smolder until you can get to them.

The multi-tasking onion of productivity lies

Here's a fun fact for you: multitasking is a scam. It's a productivity onion with layers of bullshit wrapped around nothing.

We think: *If I can manage five tasks at once, I must be five times as productive.*

It's not true; this is a mental fabrication sold to us by our ambition, and occasionally stuffed down our throats by a corporate culture that praises the *hustle.*

Our brains are not wired for multitasking. Neuroscientists have found that when we think we are multitasking, we are actually rapidly switching attention from one task to another. This constant switching costs us: mental fatigue, errors, and, ultimately, the quality of each individual task.

While Ego feeds your delusions about multitasking, your brain, the Ferrari of cognitive machinery, actively gets downgraded to a clunky, 20-year-old Toyota struggling with stop-and-go traffic (I could have said a Fiat, but you know, I'm Italian, and we love Fiat).

Imagine your brain as a laser beam.

What happens when you diffuse that beam? It loses its cutting power. Now, imagine focusing that beam on a single task. It cuts through a piece of metal with precision and speed. That's the power of *uni-tasking*: bringing all your horsepower to one endeavor at a time.

In a sense, uni-tasking breaks the illusion of productivity. This less-is-more approach derives from a profound understanding of your cognitive limitations and the courage to stray from conventional wisdom for something less sexy but far more effective.

Richard Koch puts it perfectly: "People are effective because they say *no*, because they say, *this isn't for me*." Apply that discernment to your tasks. Choose what deserves your focus. Say *no* to the allure of multitasking and *yes* to the effectiveness of singular attention.

Messi's way and the value of your time

In 2023, David Beckham, the now-retired superstar footballer and current owner of Inter Miami, was asked about advice that his new mega signing Lionel Messi had offered to youngsters in the Miami team.

The podcasters hosting the interview were your average over-enthusiastic Yanks salivating at the thought of the click-baity, over-the-top answer that could have come from an influential owner while marketing his star signing.

In a way, they did get a fantastic response because Mr. Beckham coyly said: "You won't believe it, but all Leo told them was, *Run less*".

If you observe Messi during any game, you will notice that he is constantly walking but rarely idle. He is looking around, scanning players and free spaces, and then, before anyone can catch up, he scores a goal or creates a potential chance primarily because of all the saved-up energy that elevates his already wizard-like skills. In fact, in a famous El Clasico match (a "clasico" is any instance of a Real Madrid-Barcelona game), a Spanish newspaper by the name *El Periodico* kept track of Messi's movement and analyzed it thoroughly. The data crunchers established that the legendary player walked nearly 83.1% of the total game time, and only sprinted for a little over 1%.

Yes: Messi sprints for about 60 seconds a match. Do you really believe that working like a mad person for 18 hours a day will give you the results you are chasing?

Naval Ravikant, the Indian-American entrepreneur and investor, CEO of AngelList, who looks like he is meditating even when he is talking, brings a refined perspective to this subject. He says you need to *value your time* like a wealthy man values his wealth.

The problem is that, often, we are wasting not just our time but also our uniqueness: Naval talks about something he calls *Specific Knowledge*, which cannot be taught in a classroom or copied by some guy handy at PowerPoint sitting three cubicles away. It's not a template, it's not a methodology, it's you. If someone else can do what you do, congratulations, you are replaceable (and if you are replaceable, you are not that valuable). The goal is to build something Naval would call your *Personal Monopoly*: the intersection of hard skills, soft skills, quirks, and knowledge so specific and so *bizarrely* you that nobody else can replicate it. The more unique your combination of skills, the more unfair edge you carry with you.

In consulting, this means automating the mundane stuff, delegating the low-value tasks, and only dedicating your energy to high-value work that compounds over time. It means figuring out how to turn your work from a linear effort-reward exchange into something that scales. You are burning your potential if you are too busy answering emails and building slides nobody asked for.

You have to stop thinking about your time as some $200-an-hour metric. It's not an hourly rate; it's a *fortune* waiting to be unlocked. It's a resource that, if used correctly, multiplies itself. Think of it like compound interest: an hour spent building a new skill, expanding your network, or perfecting your craft today could translate into hundreds of thousands of dollars in revenue down the line. The point is not to just get better at your job. The point is to become the person whose job cannot be replaced. If you want to do that, you must start valuing your time like it's the last water bottle in a desert.

Let me share a personal experience.

Years ago, I was still early in my career and hustling my way through the London consulting scene. I went to a networking event, the kind where everyone is one bad cocktail away from crying about their boss. I struck up a conversation with this South African executive, an older guy, sharp as hell, whose presence alone seemed to quiet the noise. We hit it off, talking about work, life, and everything in between. By the night's end, he offered me a job, just like that. Unfortunately, I had just moved to my firm at the time, and it was too soon for me to jump ship, so I politely declined. We kept in touch for a while, but the connection eventually faded like most professional relationships do. Fast forward eleven years. I walked into my office in Australia... and there he was. The same South African executive, freshly hired into the senior leadership team. We stared at each other before he burst out laughing: "Well, looks like I ended up following you instead!"

The moral of the story is that networking is not about instant gratification but about planting seeds and letting them grow on their timeline. When they do grow, they often bear fruit where you least expect it.

How do you actually build this irreplaceable, one-of-a-kind *Personal Monopoly*? It's simple: you make yourself incomparable. You learn skills nobody else has, form relationships nobody else can duplicate, and work in ways nobody else can match.

Take an hour every day to build your talent stack: the skills that make you both uniquely valuable and ridiculously hard to replace. Learn things that are tangential to your core consulting work. Become the best in your firm at visual storytelling, or the go-to expert on some niche technology nobody else can wrap their head around. Create a network of people who would take your call at 2 am because they know you are worth listening to.

Nine-tenths of wisdom is being wise in time. The smartest people in the world are not necessarily the hardest working, but they are the most *selective* with their time; they guard it like a vicious dog protects a bone, because they know that wasted time is wasted potential. You have to be brutal about what you choose to work on. If something is not serving your growth, you kill it. Ruthlessly.

The goal is not to be busy but to be effective.

Start seeing your time as a non-renewable resource. Invest it with the same intensity you would invest a million dollars.

Over the long term, the returns are far more significant.

***

Vignette

The office is half-empty. Ivy is hunched over her desk, eyes glazed, aimlessly scrolling through an Excel sheet. Morrie walks past, coat over his shoulder, an apple ginger juice in hand. He stops.

Morrie: Still here?
Ivy [not looking up]: Obviously. Got a million things to do. This client is a nightmare. Every little thing is "urgent." Every email, every slide. I feel like I am drowning.
Morrie: Let me ask you something. Have you ever watched Messi play?
Ivy [blinks, confused]: Uh... yeah, I did actually.
Morrie: What is the first thing you notice?
Ivy: I mean... he is fast? Skilled?
Morrie: Wrong. He walks. 80% of the game, he is just walking. Watching. Finding angles. He moves *less*, so that when he does move, he is precisely where he needs to be. In consulting, my friend, you want to be Messi.
Ivy [leans back, rubbing eyes]: You are saying I should *walk* more?
Morrie: I am saying you are running in circles because you think movement equals progress. It does not. 80% of what you are doing right now is pretty much useless. The trick is knowing which 20% actually matters.
Ivy [gesturing to laptop]: So what, I just stop answering emails? Ignore half my tasks?
Morrie [shrugs]: Cut out the fluff. Say no to the meetings that do not need you. Summarize your points in two slides instead of twenty. You will get more done by doing *less*.
Ivy: And what if my boss asks why I am not running all over the pitch like an idiot?

Morrie: Simple. Just tell them you are playing like Messi.

Morrie stands, pats Ivy's desk, and strolls off. Ivy watches him go, then slowly, almost reluctantly, reaches for the mouse... and closes half her open tabs.

***

Practical exercises

To practice the key ideas discussed in this chapter, work on the following three actionable exercises:

The 80/20 diary

Activity: For one week, keep a diary of all your work tasks and how much time you spend on each. Review your diary at the end of the week, and identify the top 20% of tasks that contributed most to your productivity and progress.

Objective: This exercise aims to help you apply the 80/20 rule to your work, allowing you to identify and focus on tasks that yield the most significant results, enhancing efficiency and effectiveness.

Time blocking trial

Activity: Plan your next workday using the Time Blocking method. Allocate specific time blocks for different tasks, ensuring you match high-priority tasks with your peak cognitive periods. Stick to this schedule as closely as possible throughout the day.

Objective: The goal is to familiarize yourself with Time Blocking, improving your ability to effectively manage and dedicate time to tasks, thereby increasing your productivity and ability to engage in deep work.

Urgent vs. Important matrix

Description: Create an Eisenhower Matrix by drawing a two-by-two grid. Label one axis "Urgent" and the other "Important." Place your weekly tasks in one of the four quadrants. Tasks that are both urgent and important go in the top-left quadrant, and so forth.

Objective: This exercise helps you prioritize tasks based on urgency and importance, teaching you to focus on what truly matters and avoid getting overwhelmed by tasks that seem urgent but are not truly important to your success or well-being.

A GLOBAL CONSULTANT KNOWS HOW TO PLAY EVERYWHERE

When Odysseus set sail from Troy, he did not expect a decade-long journey home filled with one-eyed giants, seductive sirens, and vengeful gods. Homer's hero had to navigate the Mediterranean while learning to adapt or die.

Today's consultant does not battle Cyclopes, but rather mustard sandwiches in London and Iowa's bone-chilling -34°C winters (more on this in a bit). Like Odysseus, who changed from warrior to beggar to king as circumstances demanded, the modern professional must shape-shift across continents and cultures. The ancients understood what business schools still don't teach: knowledge is not primarily theoretical, but experimental, gained through what Seneca called *hardship* (you might have heard the expression *per aspera ad astra*). That's why your MBA syllabus will not mention how to navigate a Hong Kong boardroom's invisible hierarchies, or why your German colleague arrives thirty minutes *early* by Italian standards...

Unlike their modern counterparts who live to enjoy life and eat lots of *pasta all'amatriciana*, the ancient Romans approached matters with gravity and discipline. They did not conquer the ancient world by forcing Latin on everyone: they absorbed the strengths of each conquered culture.

Your career conquest requires the same tactical flexibility.

Navigating the globe has always been a thrill and a complexity in my consulting journey. Whether it's the marble-floored halls of Fortune 500 companies in the USA, red-eye flights to Sydney, or bustling Asian *wet markets*, each new time zone and local SIM card has added a new layer to my professional make-up.

I have spent most of my years living abroad, outside of my home country, Italy: this meant I had to adapt quickly to constantly changing homes, habits, and circles of friends.

To be frank, it wasn't easy.

Starting afresh in an unfamiliar territory is a formidable challenge, and managing the isolation that comes with such changes requires constant adaptation and growth. No matter how much you romanticize it, leaving behind the familiar comforts of your established world for the unknown is daunting.

I started university at 17, a good 1,200 kilometers away from home, like some overly ambitious nomad chasing education instead of sheep. Then came the consulting life and its relentless cycle of packing up, moving cities, and hitting the reset button on my life so many times that it felt like I was playing a cruel game of Monopoly.

Moving from Italy to the UK without speaking English was like deciding to become a sushi chef after spending your entire life making pizza. I was fluent in espresso, hand gestures, tomato passata, and Dante, but none of that helps when your boss emails you in corporate English and expects you to reply without Google Translate. Most people improve their English by reading textbooks. I did it by burning my boats: throwing myself into a country where I could not order a sandwich without a panic attack. Paradoxically, that made it stick, because survival is a better teacher than school.

Learning English was about optionality: once you speak the *lingua franca* of capitalism, you no longer belong to one country. You belong to the world. You unlock a global lattice of knowledge, jokes, contracts, arguments, network and backroom deals that your native tongue could never reach. Fluency expanded my vocabulary as well as that luck surface we spoke about in Chapter 1.

So, yes, it was a terrible plan, and precisely because it was a terrible plan, it worked.

The trouble began immediately, during my first week in London when I made the fatal mistake of trusting my British colleagues' food recommendations. They raved about this so-called "sandwich shop" as if it were a cathedral of culinary excellence. What they failed to mention was that the place should have been marked with asterisks, footnotes and a health warning for anyone raised on a diet of burrata, prosciutto San Daniele, and dignity.

Day One. I ordered the first sandwich I saw on the menu. A complete disaster. The thing was slathered in mustard like it had been baptized in yellow napalm. My taste buds went into shock. In Italy, we treat food like art. This monstrosity was performance art, and the message was: *Suffer.* The plastic-tasting bread did not help either. It was like someone tried to make bread by asking an algorithm what food should taste like.

Day Two. I was ready. I walked into that place like a gladiator into the Colosseum. I would not be humiliated again. I went straight to the waitress and spelled out my order in broken but determined English:

"No mustard, please." I should have received a standing ovation: I had delivered my lines with confidence. Instead, the lady at the counter looked at me like I had just proposed marriage in hieroglyphics. She asked me something. I had no idea what it was. Must be her accent, I thought. "No mustard," I repeated, my voice quivering slightly but still fighting the good fight. She didn't look satisfied. And then she repeated the exact phrase, with the same unintelligible accent, which might as well have been Silbo Gomero at that point.

My palms started sweating; my cheeks turned red. Panic started bubbling up from my stomach like the bad cappuccino from the Caffe Nero next door. The voice of doom crept into my head: *You have been here a week and can't even communicate with the sandwich lady. And you think you are going to make it professionally? Pack up and go back to Italy. The only English you need is "Mamma mia, I failed."*

Desperation took over. I summoned all my courage and stammered, "Yes, I don't want mustard." A sentence so devoid of meaning it should have collapsed into a black hole of stupidity right then and there. The lady stared at me like I had just lost a fight against a piece of toast. Her eyes burned with the specific fury of someone forced to have an interaction they know will be retold to their friends later that evening as a tragicomic anecdote. Finally, in an act of mercy or spite (I am still not sure which), she grabbed a slice of white bread in one hand and a slice of brown bread in the other. She waved them in the air like evidence at a murder trial and shouted, "WHITE BREAD OR BROWN BREAD?"

Oh. Ohhhhh. All the blood drained from my face as I realized the cruel absurdity of the situation. Here I was, in the middle of Chiswick, delivering a full-blown Shakespearean performance about mustard while the poor woman was just trying to figure out if I wanted white or brown bread. I muttered something along the lines of "white bread," my voice the consistency of melted gelato.

As I walked away with my sandwich of shame, I realized something: when you are the outsider, the immigrant, the non-native, you either adapt fast or become the punchline of someone else's story.

The trick is to take that embarrassment, bottle it, and use it as fuel. I had two options: drown in humiliation or turn it into a motivator. I chose the latter. That was the last time I made the mistake of not asking clarifying questions.

Also, it was the last time I ordered a sandwich in that place.

Cultural Arbitrage lets you play two games at once

One of the most transformative experiences of my career came when I worked in Hong Kong, a city that takes the concept of speed, dips it in Red Bull, and forces it through a maze of neon lights and dragon statues. If you have lived there, you know exactly what I am talking about. And if you have not, well, you are missing out on Earth's most mind-boggling chaos.

I call it *Cultural Arbitrage*: the art of exploiting your understanding of local customs and behavioral nuances to transform yourself into an irresistible consulting professional beyond your technical skills. You learn to sell your ability to navigate foreign territory like a linguistic and cultural mercenary.

Hong Kong's business culture is a bizarre cocktail of the hyper-formal and the hyper-fast. You bow to hierarchy, but you better be damn quick about it. Respect is mandatory; hesitation is a liability. The locals speak a language of efficiency and hierarchy so fluently that your Western playbook might as well be written in crayon. Imagine being a 26-year-old consultant thrown into Asia's largest insurance transformation project. That was me. Fresh off the plane just landed from Heathrow Airport, armed with a platinum Hyatt membership and the smug assumption that what worked in London would work anywhere. Spoiler alert: it did not. Not even close.

The hustle of situational fluency

The trick about *Cultural Arbitrage* is that it teaches you *Situational Fluency*, the ability to adapt your communication style, problem-solving approach, and leadership tactics depending on the environment. It is like developing a sixth sense for reading the room before you even walk into it. I learned quickly that if I wanted to thrive, I had to ditch the arrogance of the *one-size-fits-all* consulting approach. No, you do not talk to a Hong Kong executive the same way you would to a London banker who just spent half the meeting pretending to care about your market insights while mostly thinking about Chelsea's next football game.

I did not get it at first.

In fact, I walked into early meetings like a well-dressed lamb into a professional slaughterhouse. One of the first times I got publicly eviscerated was during a presentation to a client's CFO and his team in Hong Kong. I showed up armed with 40 slides, speaking rapid-fire English in a thick Italian accent, like I was auctioning off at the Pompeii market.

Ten minutes in, I was building up to a brilliant insight (at least, brilliant in my head) when a senior exec stopped me cold. The guy was a machine. Born and bred in Hong Kong, worked 20 hours a day (not making this up), and somehow still had time to show up every morning in a tailor-made suit with a peacock-colored pocket square, a perfect shave, and shoulder-length hair that made him look even more intimidating.

He would always make me feel underdressed, underprepared, and under-evolved in one glance. He leaned back, arms crossed, no emotion in his face, and said: "So what's your point?" No smile, no warning whatsoever, absolutely no recognition of the twelve hours I had spent aligning bullet points for him. And that is when it hit me: nobody cares about the craft if it misses the context.

I had built the perfect cathedral of irrelevance. They did not want my analysis. They wanted a conclusion. Sharp. Actionable.

In the West, you might get away with a bit of theater, some charisma, a clever quote, a graph nobody understands but everyone nods at. In Asia, I found the bullshit detector to be military-grade. If you cannot articulate exactly why you are talking, and what they are supposed to do about it, you are wasting their time and almost insulting them.

The "so what?" is not a rhetorical flourish. It is the sword hanging above your neck. Everywhere in the world this question matters, of course, but here, it is existential.

Lead with usefulness. Earn the right to be heard. If there is any patience for flash, it only comes after you have proven you are not ornamental. That is when I started paying attention. I watched the locals and the expats who thrived. I started mimicking, not their accents, but their rhythm. I learned to speak in value per sentence, not value per deck. I got used to pausing when it mattered and dropping the clever phrasing to go straight to utility. I started to frontload insights like those street vendors selling watches in Causeway Bay: fast and in your face, because the customer is already halfway down the block.

Once you crack the code, you become something else: no longer just another consultant but a translator between worlds. And being a translator makes you valuable in ways that transcend your technical skills.

The global rolodex effect and the hardship premium

There is a side effect to mastering *Cultural Arbitrage,* and it is called the *Global Rolodex Effect.* As a young consultant, you are essentially a sponge with an expense account, soaking up every experience you can. More importantly, you are building a network that crosses borders. These people are not just LinkedIn connections or obligatory Christmas card recipients. They are allies. They are doors waiting to be opened, years later, when you least expect it. Some of them will drop you a message asking for a favor. Some will vouch for you in rooms you are not even aware exist. And some will pop up on the other side of the planet just when you need them the most.

Want proof? I once struck up a casual conversation with a guy in a Hong Kong pub near the Jockey Club. It turns out he was an executive at a UK-based insurance, seconded in Asia. A few years later, he introduced me to a client who turned into a seven-figure contract for the firm I was working for at the time. And all I did was ask him about his favorite beer garden in Happy Valley.

There is also a darker and more brutal lesson. I call it the *Hardship Premium* (figuratively, but also literally: many firms offer financial incentives for taking international assignments). Making a few extra bucks back in Hong Kong (which is always lovely), meant I had to work from 7 am to 10 pm, 6 days a week. Yes, it was ridiculous, borderline criminal, pure masochism dressed in business casual. But it was helpful. It taught me to view the *normal* 9-to-5 workday as a joke, like a vacation. When you push yourself beyond what you think is your limit, you expand your capacity for stress. You become more resilient, efficient, and dangerous as a player. Call it *grit*, call it *insanity*, the result is the same: you become a weapon. When you return to more conventional projects, you will chew through them like a machine that has tasted blood and wants more. Here's where it gets real, though.

All of this, the Cultural Arbitrage, the Global Rolodex, the Hardship Premium, becomes *leverage*, and leverage is the closest thing to power that a young consultant can get. These are not just nice stories to put on your CV. They are negotiation chips. If you are not using them to demand better projects, higher pay, or broader opportunities, then (excuse my French) what the fuck are you even doing?

If you are smart, you will weaponize these experiences. Thomas Edison said, "Genius is 1% inspiration and 99% perspiration," but in consulting, that sweat gets squeezed out in unfamiliar airports, lost translations, and meetings where you are the least understood person in the room. What you gain is adaptability under fire that no classroom or online course can simulate. That is the real education: delivered one cultural misstep, one jetlagged breakthrough at a time.

Did I ever tell you about my stint working in the United States of America? I thought I was off to live the New York dream (strutting down Manhattan like some big deal out of a GQ spread), but no, life had other plans. Instead of being dazzled by city lights, I found myself freezing my ass off in Des Moines, Iowa. For those unfamiliar with the American Midwest, Des Moines is the place where *urban* means two Starbucks on the same street and "exotic cuisine" means putting hot sauce on your cheeseburger. It's where personal fitness means finding the closest drive-through, and socializing involves oversized plates of bacon and pancakes that look like NASA engineered them. It felt like I had accidentally been signed up for a field study in anthropological absurdity. Before moving there, the only thing I knew about Iowa was from *Field of Dreams*, that movie where Kevin Costner builds a baseball field in the middle of a cornfield because some disembodied voice tells him, "If you build it, he will come." Shoeless Joe Jackson, a ghostly baseball player, arrives, looks around, and asks, "Is this heaven?" To which Ray responds: "No, it's Iowa."

Iowa. Hell's own refrigerator.

Temperatures are so cold they should be illegal: we are talking about *-34°C* (-29°F) during the day. And this was not some Nordic, romantic winter wonderland but soul-crushing, eyeball-freezing, face-numbing misery. Walking from the parking lot to the office took approximately one minute, just long enough to lose all sensation in my forehead and question every life decision that brought me to the frozen gut of the American Midwest. For someone raised under the Italian sun, who had already sworn off Arctic misery after a short, delusional stint in Reykjavik five years earlier, where I spent a winter eating rotten shark and consulting for a bank that promptly went belly-up in the global financial crisis (pure coincidence, I swear), Iowa felt like Dante's Ninth Circle of Hell, only with more cornfields and far fewer poets.

The thing about Iowa is that walking is considered an exotic and suspicious activity. Something is wrong with you if you are not encased in a metal box on wheels. I am not just talking about the insane number of cars. I am talking about drive-through everything.

A drive-through Starbucks. A drive-through petrol station. A drive-through food joint. A drive-through ATM, for God's sake!

The whole state is designed to accommodate people who want to experience life without the inconvenience of standing up.

The food portions are massive: you order a meal, and it feels like you are receiving a peace offering from a hostile nation. The tipping culture is crazy: the European mind truly cannot comprehend why you must pay extra to prevent your waiter from plotting your demise.

Moving to Iowa in my early 30s felt less like a career decision and more like a *psychiatric episode*. Why the hell would I leave a thriving European city for the frozen cornfields of America's Heartland? Well, because it was America, damn it. If you want to understand the world's economic superpower, you must roll up your sleeves and dive into the insanity.

Working in Iowa made me better at my job (yes, the same job that had me puzzled about my work life every time I scraped frost off my car windshield). When you genuinely want to understand corporate America, you do not learn it from a cushy office in Manhattan; you learn it from places like Des Moines, where people work hard, talk straight, and think an avocado toast is something rich people invented to mess with the common man.

Americans, especially in the Midwest, appreciate detailed, vivid stories with real-life examples. They do not want to hear your abstract frameworks or high-concept jargon when you talk business with them. They want something that feels real. I learned that, when dealing with American offices and clients, your European-style restraint and obsession with technical precision will only get you so far. You must loosen up, embrace the narrative, and speak their language.

In practice, this means anchoring your pitch in a real story. "We had this client in Ohio, running a $20M distribution business, margins razor-thin, tech stack from the Stone Age. Here's what we did..."

That kind of story will get more attention than ten Harvard frameworks stacked on top of each other. The moment they see themselves in your example, they start listening. They will not care how clever your model is, but they will care whether you understand their mess, and whether you have cleaned up something similar before.

In America, a story is a communication tool and a trust accelerator, a way to pass the bullshit test without sounding like a know-it-all. And when the world runs on dollars, *learning how to speak the language of the dollar* is pure survival.

Now, do not get me wrong. In many ways, Iowa was a circus of absurdity, but I did not let the experience go to waste. I extracted every ounce of value from the ordeal: I was right in the middle of America, after all! I visited Johnny Cash's museum in Nashville, Tennessee, just to feel the presence of a man who turned pain into gold. I stood outside Warren Buffett's house in Omaha, Nebraska, just to see where a man worth hundreds of billions chooses to live like a frugal monk. I drove through the Eight Mile in Detroit with my Californian friend *Shrimpin'* Eddie from Stockton (he grew up on noodles and seafood in the most dangerous city in America, hence the nickname), and we felt like two rappers minus the talent and the trauma. I also ate the best ribs of my life in Kansas City, a meal so glorious I nearly wept. Yes, I froze my butt off. Yes, I cursed my luck for not landing a fancier engagement somewhere that did not involve the threat of frostbite. But when I look back, I realize that my time in the Midwest was an exercise in *Cultural Arbitrage.*

Now, when I deal with American clients, I have a crystal-clear understanding of how they think, what they value, and how to talk to them in a way that actually moves the needle. And I know that if I can survive Iowa, I can survive anything.

The cross-cultural fitness edge is hard to get

You know what's more complicated than cracking a multi-million-dollar client account? Not looking like a clueless idiot when you are thrown into a foreign business culture and expected to perform like some cross-continental consulting god. You might think a quick Google search about local customs and a few *ciao* and *ni hao* sprinkled into conversation will do the trick, and you would be wrong: it most definitely won't.

Navigating cross-cultural business situations with finesse is not some corporate brochure nonsense about *global integration*. It's learning how not to humiliate yourself and still, when you inevitably do, learning how to recover fast enough to make it look like you meant to do that. When you nail it, you go from being that awkward foreigner everyone quietly feels sorry for, to the guy they want in the room. Your presence goes from triggering polite nods to nods of respect.

Nobody tells you that culture is *not* just food, language, or public holidays. It's how people communicate, make decisions, and even view something as simple as *time*. Culture is everything you do, especially the stuff you do unconsciously. When you get it wrong, you embarrass yourself, plus you actively damage your credibility.

For instance, let's talk about hierarchy. In some Eastern cultures, hierarchy is an unwritten law. You cannot just walk into a conference room, slap your laptop open, and dive right into the agenda. There is a whole ritual: who speaks first, who gets the prime seat at the table, and who gets to challenge an idea openly. Now try that same approach in Northern Europe, where everyone is on a first-name basis and the guy in sweatpants and sneakers could be the CEO. Act like a hierarchy-obsessed corporate samurai and they will think you are either arrogant or severely lacking in emotional intelligence (based on my Icelandic experience, there is no greater cultural whiplash than jumping from East Asia to Northern Europe).

The real comedy begins when you throw *time* into the mix. Because time, my dear consultant, is not a universal concept. It's more like an abstract painting. Everyone sees something different and insists their interpretation is correct.

In Germany, being late is like wearing Crocs to a funeral. A 2 pm meeting means you are already there at 1:50 pm, mentally prepared, laptop ready, pen in hand. Efficiency is God, and everything else is a distraction.

Now, let's take a trip to my homeland: Italy. In Italy, a 2 pm meeting can mean anything between 2:15 pm and 2:45 pm. You are expected to warm up into the meeting. Exchange pleasantries. Maybe talk about your weekend or the AC Milan game. Time is a more fluid concept.

It was amusing to experience this during one of my projects in Milan. My client was the Italian office of a bank headquartered in Germany, and I used to have many colleagues, clients, and external advisors from Germany working there. One day, my colleague and good friend Sonja from Cologne decided to show up for her 3 pm meeting at 2:50 pm. So there she was, the only person in the building drinking a cappuccino after noon (a cardinal sin in Italy), sitting alone in a meeting room twiddling her thumbs. The Italian team finally strolled in around 3:20 pm, looking amused rather than apologetic, while Sonja looked like she was seconds away from launching a formal protest to the European Union. To the Italians, her strict punctuality made her look uptight and unadaptable. To her, their casual disregard for the clock was pure madness. Both of them were right. Both of them were wrong. That's how culture works. And if you are unaware of it, you are wrong *everywhere*.

Mastering these cultural nuances is a career superpower. You cannot list it on your performance review, but it shows up in the results you deliver. It shows up when you are the one who can defuse a tense negotiation with a well-placed joke or when you know exactly how much small talk is necessary before jumping into business. It shows up when clients from across the globe ask for you by name because you are the one who *gets it.*

And when you are the consultant who can work with the New York suits, the Tokyo hierarchies, the Milanese chaos, and the Icelandic egalitarianism all in the same week, you are a translator of worlds.

As Confucius said, "Real knowledge is to know the extent of one's ignorance." That's the dirty secret of this whole game. The more you learn about navigating cultural landscapes, the more you realize how much you do not know. And that's a good thing. That's how you stay sharp for the long haul.

Every time you land a project in a new cultural setting, it's a tuition fee for your real-world MBA. Yeah, you will screw up. Yeah, the jet lag will be heavy (but you will learn that a few liters of rum & coke and listening to *Red lights indicate doors are secured* by Arctic Monkeys on loop can do wonders). You will get lost in translation, step on toes, and probably spend more time apologizing than doing actual work. But every blunder is a lesson, and every lesson is a weapon you can use.

You will be collecting war stories to share at dinner parties and first dates, and you will be the one with the best anecdotes when your friends complain about their boring corporate gigs. Build a career that feels like an adventure rather than just another paycheck, and become the envy of those stuck in their cultural bubbles.

On to the next lesson.

***

Vignette

Morrie is making instant coffee badly. Ivy storms in, wearing a jacket three sizes too big and clutching a paper bowl that smells faintly... meaty.

Morrie: You look like a tourist who tried to blend in and got outed by a stew.
Ivy: I just tried ordering lunch at that little corner place near the station. Long story short: I may have caused a minor diplomatic fallout.
Morrie: You did not ask the clarifying question, did you?
Ivy: I *thought* I was being clear! I said "no meat" three times! Turns out... they were just confirming whether I wanted small or large.
Morrie: Congratulations. You have learned the first rule of Cultural Arbitrage: in a new country, you are not misunderstood. You are stupid until proven otherwise.
Ivy: Harsh.
Morrie: Accurate. Every mistake abroad is either tuition for your global MBA or a starring role in someone's comedy night.
Ivy: So what you are saying is... I bought a beef stew as a teaching moment?
Morrie: Exactly. Cheap price for a hard lesson. Now next time, listen twice, speak once. And for God's sake, pack your own lunch.

Morrie sips his awful coffee, grimacing. Ivy pokes at the stew, watching a mystery chunk surface like it knows what it did.

***

Practical exercises

To practice the key ideas discussed in this chapter, work on the following three actionable exercises:

Cultural immersion plan

Activity: Choose a country or culture that interests you, or that you expect to work with in the future. Research its business etiquette, communication styles, and social norms. Create a plan for how you would adapt your work approach to fit into this new setting, considering meetings, presentations, and daily interactions.

Objective: This exercise aims to enhance your cultural awareness and adaptability, effectively preparing you to navigate and respect different cultural contexts, thereby improving your global professional interactions.

Situational role-play

Activity: Role-play a business scenario involving a cultural misunderstanding or challenge with a colleague or mentor, such as a meeting with international clients or a negotiation with partners from another culture. Swap roles and perspectives to see the situation from multiple angles.

Objective: The goal is to develop empathy and understanding of different cultural perspectives, improving your ability to communicate and negotiate across cultures while recognizing and respecting cultural differences.

Global networking initiative

Activity: Identify and reach out to three professionals from different cultural backgrounds within or outside your organization. Schedule informal virtual coffee chats to learn about their work experiences, cultural challenges, and insights.

Objective: This exercise aims to expand your global professional network and expose you to diverse perspectives, enhancing your cultural capital and your understanding of international business practices.

No one gets promoted for following the recipe

Imagine your *nonna* hands you her sacred ragù recipe, the one she has been perfecting since before you were born. You follow it to the letter: chop the onions just so, brown the meat precisely as she says, let it simmer for hours until your kitchen smells like a tiny trattoria in Naples. The result is a solid, respectable ragù. But does it *feel* like yours? Not really! This is nonna's sauce, nonna's wisdom, nonna's soul poured into that pot. You just followed the script.

Now, imagine you start tweaking it. Maybe a splash more red wine (because why not?), a pinch of nutmeg like they do in Bologna, a cheeky bit of Calabrian chili for a kick. Suddenly, it is no longer her ragù: it is *your* ragù.

Consulting works the same way (without the mince but with plenty of stirring). The real magic happens when you *own* the work, when you take what you see around you, add your twist, and serve something that has *your* signature on it. No one remembers the guy who just follows the recipe. They remember the one who makes it *sing*.

Day-to-day consulting relies significantly on trusted methods, dependable frameworks, and a holy grail of *best practices* that one is expected to scale and tweak across different projects, industries, and even geographies. Many times, this conventional approach can be a double-edged sword. While it offers a sense of control and repeatability, it also reveals a quiet truth we rarely admit out loud: there is very little that is genuinely *new under the sun* (the Bible knew it all along: *ein hadash tachat hashemesh*). Most of what we call innovation is often a rebranded version of old wine in a new PowerPoint slide.

We keep cycling through templates, renaming the same ideas, pitching the same "technology roadmap" dressed up for whatever trend is in vogue. The danger is that familiarity begins to masquerade as insight. We stop questioning and we start recycling. Before long, we are not solving problems but replicating patterns.

This is not the right way to interpret our profession.

Sometime early in my career, when I still had a full head of hair, I was working on a 9-figure project for the largest life insurance company in Asia. I was surrounded by established subject matter experts who constantly exchanged lively insights and feedback. During one meeting, as we continued brainstorming and drafting a plan for our engagement, I could not shake off the feeling that we were taking a tad too conventional an approach and might have an opportunity to tackle the project more creatively and differently.

At the helm of the technology side of things were two men who could not have been more different in background, yet seemed to share the same rigid, by-the-book philosophy when it came to execution.

One was an American, Bill, who looked like he had stepped straight out of a corporate IT handbook. He was in his mid-50s, short and slightly hunched from years of leaning over conference tables and laptop screens, with a receding hairline that he tried to compensate for with a meticulous comb-over. He wore rimless glasses that perched on the edge of his nose, giving him a perpetually skeptical expression, as if everything you said needed to pass a rigorous stress test before he would even acknowledge it. His wardrobe consisted exclusively of pressed blue and white shirts with starched collars, always paired with pleated khakis and a leather belt that looked like it had been through multiple promotions. Bill spoke in clipped, authoritative sentences, favored bullet points over discussions, and had an almost religious devotion to methodologies that had been written a decade earlier.

Then there was Rajiv, the Indian counterpart, who was about a decade younger but carried himself with the same measured certainty. He had a neatly trimmed mustache that framed a mouth rarely seen smiling, and he dressed in impeccably ironed light-colored dress shirts with a pen clipped to his front pocket. Unlike Bill, who leaned into American corporate informality, Rajiv was all about formality and precision. His hair was jet black and parted with military precision, and he spoke in a deep, measured tone that brooked no interruptions. While Bill was the type to shoot down new ideas with an exasperated sigh, Rajiv would do it with a slow, deliberate shake of his head, as if the mere suggestion of deviating from the plan was mildly disappointing. He had built his career on rigor: structured processes, exhaustive documentation, a belief that "the right way" was usually the way it had always been done.

Between the two of them, they commanded the technology approach with an air of unshakable certainty. While their experience was undeniable, I could not help but wonder if their insistence on staying within familiar boundaries was limiting the full potential of what we could achieve.

I actually loved both of them. They were my friends, yet I kept thinking, *Why can't we approach consulting projects like a start-up approaches product development?* This was the late 2000s, I was 25 years old, and I was vigorously reading about new internet companies. The web was taking off, and Silicon Valley start-ups were the hottest thing around (20 years later, they still seem to be!).

Let's talk start-ups

When running a rapidly scaling business, you do not have the luxury of relying on proven models and the wisdom of "best practices". You must be agile, adaptive, stringent, and innovative at every step.

There are no established norms because you are creating a niche of your own and building something that did not exist before. You can ask for advice and learn from seasoned mentors, but in the end, it's all *you*. You have to figure it out.

What if consultants across levels adopted the mindset of a start-up CEO?

Start-up CEOs must consider everything from customer acquisition to product development and team management.

Transpose those responsibilities into a consulting context, and you are playing with something intriguing.

As a consultant, you do not simply deal with your day-to-day deliverables, but you also constantly consider how to best *acquire* (engage) your client, develop a *product* (the project outcome), and manage your internal *team* (other consultants or client staff).

If you only focus on *delivery*, the numbers, and the metrics, you are missing out on many development opportunities, and you will not make it far. You are cutting yourself short.

"Your work is going to fill a large part of your life, and the only way to be truly satisfied is to do what you believe is great work," said Steve Jobs during his famous commencement speech at Stanford MBA in 2005.

Many young consultants struggle to find a purpose in this industry.

In all honesty, not every consulting engagement improves society. Some are commercially driven with little broader benefit, and others, like cost-cutting programs that quietly gut essential services, can do real harm when handled carelessly or without integrity.

However, treating each assignment as a window to novel opportunities for personal development can be a source of satisfaction.

In fact, great work and personal satisfaction need not always involve a grassroots impact on society. They can also involve achieving individual milestones, experimenting with new methodologies, mentoring less experienced peers, or, if you start drinking the Kool-Aid early enough, *maximizing shareholder value.*

In *The War of Art*, Steven Pressfield shared his thoughts around this principle more eloquently than I could ever do. He wrote:

> "Do I really believe that my work is crucial to the planet's survival? Of course not. But it's as important to me as catching that mouse is to the hawk circling outside my window. He's hungry. He needs a kill. So do I."

How do you go about adopting a start-up mindset, then?

For starters, think MVP (Minimum Viable Product). In start-up lingo, this refers to the most basic version of your product that still meets the consumer's needs.

In a consulting scenario, an MVP could be the simplest yet most effective solution for your client's problem.

Your approach should be to start lean. Provide a basic model, the absolute bare minimum that gets the message across, and iterate it based on constant feedback and results. This lean thinking is helpful in long-term projects where you have time to refine your approach.

These days, you may find people denying the value of MVP and even questioning its entire usefulness. Ignore them. They are probably talking about MVPs which were never minimum and likely not viable anyway. It would be like denigrating football (some mistakenly call it *soccer*) as a sport because you can't play like Ronaldo. Respectfully, it's not the game. It's your skills.

In the start-up world, you pivot. If something is not going right, you change course quickly. And in consulting, we could make great use of such an agile approach. Let's translate this concept to the mazes of boardrooms, Excel spreadsheets, and PowerPoint presentations.

Picture yourself knee-deep in a tech strategy project. The client has paid obscene amounts of money for a roadmap that will supposedly transform their technology landscape and, ultimately, their business. Being the diligent consultant you are, you have spent weeks refining it, aligning it to industry trends, and making the slides look like something Michelangelo himself would admire. Then, three days before the final presentation, someone from the client side (usually a guy with a title like *Chief Digital Visionary Evangelist*) leans back in his chair and says: "You know what? This is great, but what we really need is a go-to-market plan for our AI product". Most consultants would panic. Some would argue, some would *circle back*, and the worst would ignore it altogether, hoping to bulldoze their way through. An *intrapreneurial* consultant knows she needs to pivot here.

She calmly nods, takes a sip of her espresso (because, of course, she never drinks that lukewarm conference room coffee, also known as *dirty water*), and without breaking stride, says: "Interesting. Let us explore how this roadmap could be a foundation for that AI strategy." Then, she rewires the whole narrative and spins up a few slides. Suddenly, the client thinks this was the plan all along.

That is the power of pivoting. It is about changing direction while making the shift look effortless. Maybe the focus should move from cost-cutting to new revenue-generation ideas. Perhaps the problem is not the strategy but the execution plan. Whatever the reason, being flexible enough to make these shifts is critical to driving the proper outcomes. In consulting, as in life, the ones who survive are not necessarily the strongest or the smartest but the ones who can change course without looking like they are changing course.

Intrapreneurship works in teams

Another essential trait of adopting a start-up mindset is understanding that the most successful leaders do not get where they are by going at it alone. Intrapreneurship, like entrepreneurship, is a team sport. Did you ever see one of those lone-wolf types in consulting? The guy who hoards information like a medieval alchemist, guarding his precious Excel models as if they contain the secrets of the universe? He refuses to delegate because "it's faster if I do it myself," which is consultant-speak for "I do not trust anyone else, and I thrive on self-inflicted misery."

This person works insane hours, burns out, and then complains about *work-life balance* while secretly feeling superior to the team he neglected. The intrapreneurial consultant is a master conductor who does not need to play every instrument but knows exactly how to get the best sound out of the orchestra. He sees his colleagues' strengths and weaknesses the way a good chef sees ingredients: he does not expect balsamic vinegar to do the job of extra-virgin olive oil, but he knows when to use each to elevate the dish. Your *employees* (other consultants, analysts, even the client's staff) are not just resources, they are your multiplier. A start-up CEO understands this instinctively: he does not personally code the app, market the product, and manage the finances. He finds the best people, puts them in the right places, and lets them do their job. The intrapreneurial consultant does the same: he builds alliances, delegates with precision, and creates an environment where people actually *want* to contribute.

Treat your team like your not-so-secret competitive advantage, and you will be amazed at how smoothly everything runs. Treat them like disposable headcount, and you will find yourself drowning in work, staring at your screen at 2 am, wondering why you ever thought consulting was a good idea.

The essence of being a start-up CEO is the willingness to take risks. Not the kind of dumb risks that land you in bankruptcy court or on the front page of the *Financial Times* for "accounting irregularities," but calculated bets with limited downside and massive upside.

There is, however, a small catch: multi-million dollar consulting projects are often led by executives who have spent their entire careers optimizing for one thing, and that is not getting fired. These people worship risk matrices and would rather add another steering committee than making an actual decision. You walk into a meeting with a game-changing idea, and suddenly you are met with blank stares and a request to "socialize the concept with stakeholders" (which, in corporate-speak, means kill it through slow suffocation). So, what do you do? You package your wild ideas in a milder context, just enough to slip past the risk-averse antibodies.

For example, if you want to suggest an aggressive digital transformation, do not call it "aggressive!" Call it a "measured transition leveraging industry standards". If you want to propose an entirely new business model, frame it as an "optimization of existing synergies."

My daughter hates broccoli, loathes it, but I know it's good for her, so I must incorporate it into her meal rotation. If she even suspects broccoli's presence on her plate, she will stage a full-scale investigation, poking around like a forensic analyst at a crime scene. One time, I tried hiding a tiny floret under a mountain of mashed potatoes: she sniffed it out in two seconds and gave me a look of pure betrayal, as if I had personally insulted her intelligence. I then got creative and started to blend it into a pasta sauce: she ate it happily, blissfully unaware. Another time, I mixed it into meatballs: not a peep of complaint. The trick was simple: broccoli, by itself, was a hard no, but if I disguised it within something familiar, there was no resistance.

The best consultants understand that corporate decision-making is like sneaking broccoli into my daughter's meals: sometimes you just need to ensure your clients do not realize what they are eating until they have already swallowed it.

And that is where intrapreneurial consultants separate themselves from the herd. As the co-founder of PayPal and notable early Facebook investor, venture capitalist Peter Thiel wrote in *Zero to One*: "Competition is for losers." He is right. The consultant who spends her days benchmarking, playing it safe, and following industry best practices is essentially the equivalent of a waiter reading off the menu: polite, functional, and utterly replaceable. Meanwhile, the intrapreneurial consultant ignores the menu altogether. She sees a client's problem, understands the root issue, and instead of asking herself: *What have other companies done?*, she asks herself: *What should this company do?* She does not fight for incremental territory in a red ocean of sameness: she builds a whole new category without competition.

Now, to be blunt, this goes beyond career advice. This is a lens through which you see the world. Life rewards the person who spots opportunities before others, who creates rather than following. You can be the consultant who dutifully implements the same frameworks everyone else uses, or you can be the exceptional one.

One makes a comfortable living. The other builds something worth remembering.

I am young: how would that work?

I can imagine you already with pitchforks defending your helplessness as a fresher: "I am just a junior consultant. I had my mother buy me a new business outfit just months ago. Act like a start-up CEO? Pfft... I don't even have the authority to change the thermostat in the office."

Yes, I hear you, but bear with me for a second.

When working at the lower rungs of the corporate ladder, you are paradoxically in a uniquely fortunate position to experiment and be creative compared to your seniors. The stakes are different for you. The rules are different, and in a way, you are not even playing the same game. Imagine a pre-revenue start-up CEO in the early stages of their venture, busy testing different product features, exploring several customer segments, or even scrapping an idea to pursue something completely different. The agility and freedom encompassing such a mindset are similar to the liberties a junior consultant enjoys. Senior Partners have decades-long relationships, established reputations, and serious revenue targets to hit. You, on the other hand, have less to lose. Therefore, you have the breathing room to experiment and offer alternative paths of thinking.

The trick is not to strut into the office declaring that everyone else is half stupid and they should follow your new revolutionary approach. That's a CLM (a Career-Limiting Move - if you have ever seen one?)

Instead, try this.

Do you have an idea that contradicts the current strategy? Frame it as an *add-on* or a *small-scale test* rather than a full-blown change in direction. Gradually build your case with data and evidence, just like a start-up CEO would when courting investors. In my experience, consulting firms are based on meritocracy. That means good ideas can come from anywhere, even the new kid just a few months in. This happens because, in our industry, what moves the needle is revenues and client satisfaction.

Period.

If your *CEO mindset* can demonstrably contribute to those, your voice will gain weight, irrespective of your title.

George Lakoff, a cognitive linguist and semiotician, argued that language does more than describing reality: it shapes it. One of his best-known examples is the phrase "tax relief," which entered the political mainstream the day George W. Bush father took office. On the surface, it sounds benign, even helpful. But hidden inside it is a full moral frame: taxes are positioned as a burden, taxpayers as victims, and those who cut taxes as saviors. Anyone who questions this logic becomes, by default, someone who wants to prolong the pain.

Of course, you do not have to like taxes to understand how dangerous this framing is. Most people do not like taxes (I know I don't) but Lakoff is not asking anyone to feel warm and fuzzy when paying their quarterly bill. What he is saying is this: the way you talk about taxes reveals what you stand for. If you say, "I hate taxes, but I pay them because I believe in pulling my weight," you are sending a signal, and that nuance matters.

In business, in consulting, in life, your reputation is not built by trashing the system but by how you *present* your thinking. You can challenge, you can question, you can even disrupt, but you have to do it in a way that shows you understand the rules before you propose better ones. The language you use is your first handshake with the world. If you frame your message poorly (like using "tax relief" and pretending contribution is oppression) you risk sounding like a free rider, the guy who walks into the country club, eats the food, plays a round of golf, and still complains loudly about the membership fee.

If you want to be taken seriously and want your ideas to stick, you have to frame them in a way that invites respect, not resistance.

Let me share a nugget-sized story to make myself clearer.

During one of the first projects in my career, working for a major oil company, a second-year analyst spotted a significant flaw in the logic of a regulatory report our firm was tasked to design and build. It was a low-key observation, almost whispered during a coffee break. It got the attention of the Practice Lead, and a couple of meetings later, that change was getting implemented.

The guy's name was Marco, from Piacenza, a person with the easy confidence of someone who knew his stuff but did not feel the need to announce it.

He had shaggy dark hair that always seemed one week overdue for a cut, and he carried the faint smell of espresso, as if he had just stepped out of a café even when he had been at his desk all day. Marco loved guitars: he could spend hours talking about vintage Stratocasters and tube amps, though his playing was mostly confined to late-night jam sessions with friends. The man could have lived on *gnocco fritto* and mortadella alone. If you so much as mentioned it, he would go off on a passionate rant about how nobody outside Emilia truly understood its perfection (if you have never heard of *gnocco fritto*, Google the dish, try it, and then you'll thank me). He embodied an unusual combination: he was sharp enough to catch a million-dollar mistake without breaking a sweat, and warm enough to spend the rest of the night arguing over whether tagliatelle should be cut by hand or machine.

Anyway, everybody praised Marco for that problem he found: showing initiative resulted in some accolades for him and eventually led to huge savings in rework for the client.

Talk about return on investment!

By continuously offering nuanced, well-thought-out ideas, you earn stripes that are not on your job description but are nonetheless visible to those who matter. Once you've got those stripes, wear them proudly.

You are the junior consultant who thinks like a CEO.

***

Vignette

Morrie is hunched over his desk, building an impossibly complicated model out of paperclips. Ivy walks in holding two pieces of paper: one neatly formatted, one scribbled with messy ideas.

Ivy: Okay. I made two versions of the strategy paper. One is the 'best practices' version. The other... is my own take.
Morrie [without looking up]: And which one do you believe in?
Ivy: Mine. But the other one feels... safer.
Morrie [sighs, setting down his paperclip sculpture]: Kid, safe is for seatbelts and condoms. Not for ideas.
Ivy: But what if they think it is too much? Too different?
Morrie: If they wanted a copy-paste job, they would have hired someone cheaper. You are here to *cook*, not microwave leftovers.
Ivy: So I pitch my own version?
Morrie [grinning]: You pitch it like it was their idea all along. Add a few "industry standard" sprinkles if you must. But never forget whose sauce it is.

Ivy looks at the messy page in his hands, a small, wicked smile spreading. Morrie nods approvingly and goes back to constructing a miniature leaning Tower of Pisa out of paperclips.

***

Practical exercises

To practice the key ideas discussed in this chapter, work on the following three actionable exercises:

MVP project proposal

Activity: Identify a small-scale problem within your current project or team operations and develop a Minimum Viable Product (MVP) experiment. Document your proposal that addresses the core issue, including the problem statement, your proposed MVP brief, and how it can be iteratively improved based on feedback.

Objective: This exercise aims to cultivate a mindset of starting lean and being open to iterative improvements, mirroring the start-up approach to product development.

Pivot simulation exercise

Activity: Reflect on a past project or develop an hypothetical scenario where things did not go as planned. Reassess the situation and propose a pivot, a strategic shift in approach or focus. Outline what the pivot would entail, how it differs from the original plan, and why it could lead to better outcomes. Share your pivot proposal with a mentor or peer for feedback.

Objective: To practice the art of flexibility and adaptability in consulting projects. This exercise trains you to avoid being overly attached to one strategy and to be open to changing course when necessary to achieve better results.

Team asset mapping

Activity: Conduct an informal assessment of your current project team or a group of peers, identifying each member's strengths, skills, and potential areas for growth. Consider how each person's attributes contribute to the team's overall capabilities, and brainstorm ways to leverage these strengths more effectively in your collective work.

Objective: This activity encourages you to view your team through the lens of a start-up CEO, recognizing the value of each 'employee' and establishing a collaborative environment where everyone's skills are utilized to their fullest potential.

USE HUMOR TO MAKE WORK SUSTAINABLE

Let me say the quiet part out loud.

The world does not need another joyless, self-important, PowerPoint-slinging consultant who thinks calling a client "challenging" is some form of intellectual courage.

We all know those people: wearing gray suits (or black skirts), rehearsed smirks, incapable of laughter unless it involves a sycophantic joke about the Partner's golf game. They think seriousness is a proxy for competence. They wear their job titles like crowns, and sign emails with more flair than a Roman senator.

Do not become that person. In fact, run in the opposite direction.

Early in your career, the best competitive edge you can cultivate, beyond all the frameworks, certifications, and jargon-fu, is *lightness*, a certain playfulness of mind, a willingness to take your work seriously without taking yourself seriously, a little foolishness, if you will.

Finding the right balance between being serious and keeping things engaging can truly make a difference. If you learn to laugh mid-crisis, name projects after Greek monsters and Roman gods, and still make your team crack up after 14 hours on Zoom, you may begin to understand that humor is not distraction but resilience in disguise.

In the late 15th century, King Matthias Corvinus ruled Hungary and Croatia with a mix of military brilliance and ruthless diplomacy. He was a feared monarch, a Renaissance intellect, and a man surrounded by sycophants. His court was full of advisors, each polished and deferential. Nobody dared challenge him. Not really. They wrapped their opinions in flattery and hedged every recommendation like a gambler hedging a doomed bet.

Except one, who we will call Janos the Fool.

Janos was the court jester: he was short, hunched, dressed in ridiculous clothes with bells on his hat and a sharp tongue honed to a razor's edge. His job was to make the king laugh, yes. But also to do something far more dangerous: tell him the truth.

One day, when the king gathered his ministers to debate whether to increase taxes to fund a lavish expansion of his palace, no one dared object. After all, Matthias had already drawn up the blueprints: he wanted a fountain shaped like a lion devouring a Turk and no one wanted to be *that guy* who told him, "maybe not now."

No one, but Janos.

He waddled into the chamber with a dead chicken tied to a stick and a silver crown on its head. Silence. Awkward looks. One minister nervously coughed. Janos bowed low and said, "Your Majesty, allow me to present your new Finance Minister."

Laughter rippled across the room, stifled, uncertain. The king narrowed his eyes. "Explain yourself, fool." And Janos, smiling sweetly, said:

"Like your ministers, this chicken is very dead but looks important. It wears a crown and says nothing. It will not argue with you. It will not challenge you. It agrees with every word. You will love it."

A pause.

Then the king burst out laughing, genuinely.

The tax was shelved, and the palace expansion was postponed.

Two weeks later, King Matthias called Janos into his private chambers and said: "Fool, you are the only one in this court I can trust, because you are the only one who tells me I am wrong, and makes me laugh while doing it."

Now, none of this ever happened because I literally invented the whole thing, but this story still has a point.

The fool was untouchable not because he was powerful but because he was *funny*. His armor was his irreverence. His superpower was levity. That is what allowed him to cut through the hierarchy without drawing blood.

In modern consulting, the equivalent of Janos is the associate who can speak plain truth in a meeting, wrapped in a smart joke, the one who can call out the emperor's new org structure, and still get invited to dinner. In this sense, humor is a delivery mechanism for truth, not a distraction from the work. Humor is authority, just earned sideways.

The piece of advice no one gives, because it sounds wrong (until you live it), is therefore: Use humor to manipulate power without anyone noticing.

In every room, power flows like electricity: invisibly, and dangerously. Most junior consultants try to plug into it by following protocol, by showing up early, nodding politely and over-preparing. They want to be trusted and taken seriously, but face a paradox. When you try to be taken seriously, you are handing over your power.

You are saying, "Please validate me."

Instead, I suggest you practice a move that seems idiotic but is actually high-status jiu-jitsu: make a joke! Make a clever, self-aware joke, one that signals you do not need the room. You say: "This is all a little absurd, and I'm smart enough to know it... and secure enough to say it out loud."
This move does two things:
1) It reorders the social hierarchy in your favor,
2) It makes people relax their guard around you.
Now you have access, not through intimidation or deference, but through human control. You pulled off a Trojan Horse for influence.

You can plant a provocative idea, a challenge to groupthink, a criticism of the current approach, and if it is wrapped in humor, it slides past everyone's defenses. Nobody attacks the joke. They laugh. But they heard it. And it lingers.

Fun is a retention strategy

My loosely held theory is that most consultants do not burn out from the hours, but from their *humorlessness*. People display such sanctimony, exhibit performative perfection, engage in self-censorship, and show a constant need to *read the room* instead of just being a fucking human being. What kept me going in the hardest projects was, yes, *grit, discipline, sleep hygiene* and all that, but also inside jokes, dumb rituals, and unsolicited memes.

Let me tell you about the time, while living in a town called Tilburg in the Netherlands, I became *Johnny*.

Tilburg, for the uninitiated, is not Amsterdam: it has no red light district, no Rembrandt, and certainly no smug cyclists in designer wool coats. It is a city of factories turned art spaces, techno gigs in abandoned warehouses, young university students with a particular taste for weird beer, and a train station that looks like it was designed by a committee who all hated each other.

I was busy there with a consulting assignment that I thought would be low-key (tidy decks, punctual trains, strong cheese and *bitterballen*), but instead gave me one of the most profound insights of my early career: the name you give at a sushi restaurant can change your professional identity.

I will explain.

There was this Japanese restaurant we used to go to obsessively, *Sushi Koi* on the Heuvelring, just a few steps away from the Mercure Hotel suites where my whole team was based. After long days of battling business processes, SAP configuration, and surviving client meetings where the slides animations outnumbered the insights, *Sushi Koi* became a holy temple, a regular haunt for me and two of my closest companions: Mohammad and Kakhaber.

Mohammad was technically from Spain. Except he was not. He was born in Morocco. Except he was not really Moroccan either. He was from Western Sahara, a place that exists in maps but not in most embassies. "My passport," he once said while sipping miso soup, "is more of a suggestion than a document. It gets me into airports, but not out of them." Mohammad had that uniquely dry humor that only comes from watching governments collapse and then redraw borders around you like bored kids with pencils. When asked where he was from, would pause dramatically and say, "It depends: who is asking, and what is their stance on colonialism?"

Kakhaber was a big guy from Tbilisi. "Georgia," he told people, "but not the one with country music and diabetes. The old one. The real one. We invented wine while your ancestors were still trying to figure out fire." We bonded over food, by which I mean we treated every meal as a form of spiritual transcendence. He was the one who introduced me to *khachapuri*, a molten bread canoe overflowing with cheese and egg, plus the comforting embrace of post-Soviet carbohydrates. "This," he used to say, biting in, "is what you eat when life has disappointed you and you do not care anymore." At *Sushi Koi*, he once calmly devoured three kilos of nigiri like a man solving a medium-sized problem. The waitress came by twice to ask if he was done. He looked up, chopsticks mid-air, and said, "I will let you know when I die." Meanwhile, Mohammad was watching him with a blend of admiration and fear. "If we were ever in a siege," he said like in the Dutch version of *Asterix and Obelix*, "I would eat my shoe. Kakhaber would eat the army."

The food was excellent at *Sushi Koi*, the service was kind, but the booking process was a bit of a bureaucratic black hole of pain. Whenever I tried to book a table and gave them my actual name (which, as we know, is a melodically complex, Italian-sounding, weird-vowel-heavy piece of Mediterranean poetry), the poor Japanese staff at *Sushi Koi* would panic.

"Can you say it again?", "Sorry, can you spell it?", "One more time?", "Ehm... is it German?"

Five minutes into a phone call, I had gone from eager consultant to accidental hostage negotiator. And so one day, in a moment of weary genius, I snapped and said: "Just call me Johnny."

I had no idea what I was unleashing. The booking got done in 10 seconds flat. "Johnny-san, 7.30 pm, confirmed."

When I told my team, they all roared with laughter. A harmless alias became folklore: *Johnny* became a spirit animal; clients overheard it once, smiled, and started using it too.

That is how I became Johnny: at meetings, on timesheets, in retrospectives, on fake test data! Even my Starbucks order said *Johnny*, and, somehow, my coffee started arriving faster. To this day, I am known as

Johnny at most of the restaurants and coffee shops I visit around the world.

I had disarmed every room I walked into. Suddenly, I was not "the consultant from London," or "the Italian guy with the name no one can say." I was Johnny, a character. Approachable. Light. Slightly absurd. Human. What began as a workaround became a signal that said: "Relax, I am not here to play corporate cosplay."

That signal changed everything. Most consultants are trained to believe that *credibility* comes from three things:

1. Speaking in frameworks.
2. Dressing like a 1990s accountant.
3. Never laughing too loud (unless the Partner does it first, of course).

Instead, I will tell you something different: real authority comes from being able to laugh at yourself, being able to slip out of the consultant mask and into something sillier, lighter, more *alive*.

The clients did not call me Johnny because they were mocking me. They called me Johnny because it made them smile, it made me accessible, it was a shared joke in a world full of sterile slides. And do you know what happened when I needed those clients to make hard decisions? They listened, not only because of logic, but because we had laughed together and had built *trust*, the old-school way.

In consulting, most people try to *build their personal brand*, which usually means inventing a polished version of themselves, i.e., a LinkedIn-shaped avatar that they *think* will be admired by others. From becoming Johnny, I learned that the most effective identity is not the most impressive one, but the most *memorable*, the most *human*, the one people feel they can laugh with over unagi rolls.

The Latin root of the word *persona* is literally "mask." Consultants wear masks, it is part of the job, but if you wear it too long, it stops being a protection and becomes a prison.

Formality is cheap. Relatability is rare.

Every team needs a little inside joke that becomes culture. If you do not have that, and every meeting feels like a cross between a tax audit and a Big Brother interview, then you are not doing it right, because what sustains a team through late nights and difficult clients is not motivational posters or off-sites in Mallorca, but the shared absurdities.

Joy is what makes work sustainable; not tequila and, definitely, not LinkedIn likes.

Be funny or be forgotten

If you are an early-career consultant and you think humor is something you should suppress until you make Partner, I have bad news: you will never make Partner.

You will likely become the guy who takes notes well or, worse, the person clients trust to do grunt work quietly. Let me break it to you gently: you are not hired for your personality, but you are remembered for it.

Nothing lights up a room like humor. Not in the "I've got a tight five minutes of McKinsey jokes" way, I mean humor as a *modus operandi*, a lens through which you see the madness of business and smile anyway.

(By the way, do you know how you recognize an ex McKinsey consultant? Don't worry, they let you know, within 20 seconds of meeting you)

Most of the corporate world is absurd, you already know this. You sit in meetings where grown adults argue about font sizes. You have witnessed three-day back-and-forths over whether to use a hyphen in *go-to-market* (I did, at least). You have created models that forecast revenue ten years into the future using numbers your boss made up last Thursday. Yet, people take it all deadly seriously. The wisest move is to do the work well, but laugh while you do it.

Not for show or brownie points, but for survival.

Humor is status-inverting

Status is currency. You feel it in room arrangements, Microsoft Teams channels, even the awkward silences when the manager joins the call. Most juniors try to climb the ladder by being agreeable, careful, and bland enough not to upset the ecosystem. Instead, real power skips the line, and humor is a line-skipper. It is, as I like to say, *status-inverting*. You make a sharp, well-timed joke in front of a Director and suddenly you are memorable.

If I can make you laugh, I have literally moved you: I have changed your state. That is powerful!

Now, for those of you who need everything clearly explained, listen closely.

This is not an invitation to become the *funny guy*. No one wants to be the intern who interrupts a budget meeting to tell a knock-knock joke about procurement. *Humor is subtle disobedience.* The kind of humor I am talking about is dry and fast: a raised eyebrow, a throwaway line that cuts like glass and is gone before anyone can object.

It signals intelligence, not clownery, while having people relax.

Your job is to be a thinking partner, someone clients can trust to not blow up their quarterly targets *and* maybe, if the moment allows, make them laugh while saving their ass. Nobody likes the guy who's always "on," the consultant who thinks every meeting needs a joke, every slide a pun, every Teams message a meme: the louder you try to be, the more people start to wonder what you are compensating for.

Years ago, on a large transformation program, I worked with a French consultant. He was slightly chubby and very eager, probably two or three years into the job. You know the type: shirt always slightly too tight, tie worn with a kind of moral obligation, not stylistic intent. Let's call him Pierre.

Pierre wanted to be liked. Badly. He wanted attention, respect, validation: basically the usual cocktail of post-grad consulting cravings. For some reason, he had decided the best route to all that was comedy. He had decided that *every business day, at exactly 2:00 pm*, he would send an email to the full project distribution list titled: "Joke of the Day".

I don't know... He thought his job was a corporate stand-up act delivered by Microsoft Outlook.

Let me add some color: this was pre-meme-culture and pre-Reddit GIF wars. Finding a new joke back then meant *research*. Pierre was probably trawling Web 1.0 joke forums between meetings. I imagined him staying up at night, scrolling through archives of dad jokes, weighing them against the sensitivities of an international team, thinking *Yes. This one. This is the one that will make the program lead think I'm indispensable.*

One issue was that the jokes were awful. I am talking about jokes that felt like they had been translated from French to English via a Serbian translator who never left his hometown.

"Why did the consultant cross the road? To align with the business objectives on the other side."

"Two tomatoes are walking down the street. One gets hit by a car. The other says, *Catch up*."

Now imagine 50 people receiving this at 2:00 pm. Every. Single. Day.

No one ever replied. Not once. Not a "Haha." Not a pity emoji. This was the sad corporate equivalent of a stand-up comic bombing at an empty bus stop. But Pierre did not stop, because Pierre thought this was his personal *brand-building exercise*, his ticket to likeability, his way into the *inner circle*, and maybe, just maybe, my radar as program lead.

It had the opposite effect.

Instead of being seen as charming or clever, he came across as *insecure* and a bit desperate, the person you would hesitate to give real responsibility to, because you are not sure whether he will deliver the work or deliver another joke about penguins in business suits.

Humor, when forced, signals neediness

And this is the lesson: humor, when it's forced, becomes cringe.

If you are delivering a daily joke email, unsolicited, to people who have not once laughed, *you are not being seen as funny*. You are being seen as the guy who cannot take a hint, and possibly cannot be trusted with anything that requires self-awareness.

Compare Pierre's daily *bombathon* to someone who cracks a single, perfectly timed joke in a client steering committee, months into a project, when everyone is tired, the tension is thick, and they need just one moment of levity to breathe again. That person gets pulled into the next project. They used humor *surgically*, not performatively.

The tragedy is, Pierre meant well, and, in a way, I respected the effort. It takes some combination of guts and delusion to hit "Send" on 87 consecutive joke emails to a team that treats you like a fax machine they never requested.

The consultant who uses humor best is trying to make something stick. They are trying to soften a blow, bring down a wall, defuse a tense moment, reframe a ridiculous situation so everyone feels slightly less insane for being part of it.

You might crack a line after someone spends five minutes asking you if the chart can be "more innovative." You might smirk after the fourth round of feedback on a slide titled "Final_v27_FINAL_THIS_ONE_REALLY_FINAL."

You do it not for attention, but for *connection*.

In behavioral psychology, this is known as *benign violation theory*: a good joke violates expectations, but in a way that still feels safe. That's what makes it funny: the gap between what is and what should be, revealed in a flash of surprise. But do not get greedy, because the moment you start forcing it, trying to be the guy who *always* has the killer line, the whole thing backfires. Now you are the one violating trust, not bending it.

If you want bonus points, make yourself the butt of the joke. This is one of the most counterintuitive insights in the business world.

The other day, while at the office, I was adjusting my standing desk, about to start attacking my email backlog, when a colleague walked by and joked: "Oh, so you're one of those people who use a standing desk. How can you even work while standing up?"

Without missing a beat, I smiled and said: "Well, to be honest, most people don't notice whether I'm standing or sitting anyway" poking fun at my height.

It got a good laugh because, well, it's true: whether I'm sitting or standing, the difference is not exactly huge! Importantly, this small joke opened up the room for connection. Self-deprecating humor, as evident in this and the Johnny's story, is like a social lubricant. It makes people comfortable and it breaks down walls: it's one of those low-status moves that can paradoxically make you more approachable and even more influential.

Why does this work?

Because most people in corporate rooms are insecure, pretending to be more confident than they are. Everyone is scared of saying the wrong thing, being judged, exposing ignorance. When you make a joke at your own expense, you are signaling: "Relax, I'm not here to eat you." You become human, and humans (when they act so) are relatable.

There is another theory I have been toying with: when you mock your own flaws, you take control of the narrative and beat people to their judgments. You show them: "I know who I am, and I am fine with it." That kind of self-awareness is rare, and rare things are valuable. This kind of humor can position you as stronger. When you make fun of yourself, you are engaging in *benign self-disclosure*. This is a psychological principle where showing vulnerability makes others more likely to trust you. Studies have shown that when someone admits to a flaw or a mistake, it humanizes them and makes them more relatable, however the trick lies in *how* you do it.

Humor is often linked with emotional intelligence, and self-deprecating humor in particular requires a good sense of timing, self-awareness, and audience awareness.

The positive reception you get from it, hinges on the way others perceive your confidence. If your humor comes across as self-aware and playful, people see you as secure and relatable, but if it's overused or comes off as too harsh, it might signal insecurity rather than confidence.

One of the psychological phenomena that explains this balance is the *pratfall effect.*

In a classic 1966 study, psychologist Elliot Aronson found that highly competent people became more likable when they made small mistakes or showed some imperfection, but the same effect did not apply to those seen as less competent. They became even less likable when they made mistakes. This is why self-deprecating humor works well in a professional setting for people who are already perceived as competent. When you show a slight weakness or make fun of yourself in a light-hearted way, it makes you appear more approachable, but if your competence is in question to begin with, too much self-deprecation can tip the scales, making you seem less capable and, in turn, undermining your authority.

Alison Fragale, Distinguished Scholar of Organizational Behavior at the Kenan-Flagler Business School, explains that for every point you gain in social cohesion (making others feel comfortable, relatable, and connected) you risk taking an equal hit to how people perceive your expertise.

It's a seesaw between warmth and credibility. Tip too far and you go from *relatable consultant* to the *clown who cannot be trusted with the budget.* Worse: your brain starts believing the jokes. You tell yourself you are the underdog long enough, and you start behaving like one. Humor has a half-life: say it too often, and it calcifies into identity.

What should we do, then?

Again, the ancient Romans come to the rescue. They used to say: *in mediō stat virtūs*, which loosely translates to "the best option lies somewhere between two extremes."

Pair a sharp, self-aware joke with deliberate silence. Crack a line, then shut up and let the room breathe. Silence signals confidence, depth, and gives people space to think or respond. If you are constantly cracking jokes or filling every moment with humor, you might start to dilute your impact.

You risk being seen as the *funny guy* rather than someone who can also command respect. Authority lives in timing, not volume: humor gets you in the room, and silence makes them lean in.

That is how you walk the line: human and credible, memorable without being ridiculous. The corporate world is a tragicomedy, and you might as well play the fool when appropriate. Because he is the only one they listen to.

***

Vignette

We are in Morrie's office, mid-morning. He is typing one-handed while holding a biscotti. Ivy walks in looking slightly flustered.

Ivy [arms crossed]: Morrie, I made a joke in a client meeting this morning and they all laughed. Now I am worried they think I am the intern who moonlights as a stand-up comic.
Morrie [sips espresso, finally looks up]: What was the joke?
Ivy: The client said the market forecast was too optimistic. I said: "So is my dating life, but we both have to pretend for now."
Morrie [smirks]: Okay, that's actually not bad.
Ivy: That's what I thought! But then the Partner gave me this... look. But I don't want to be the funny one. I want to be taken seriously.
Morrie: Then here's your problem. You still think humor and seriousness are opposites. Humor, when used precisely, is how serious people move the room without barking. If you want power, influence, trust, then use humor. Carefully. Strategically.
Ivy: But when? How do I know if I'm overdoing it?
Morrie: You know you are doing it right when people start laughing... and listening. You know you have gone too far when they laugh and stop taking notes. Next time, recalibrate.
Ivy [smiles]: You ever make a joke that backfired?
Morrie [leans back]: I once told a client their AI roadmap looked like it was written by ChatGPT after three bottles of wine. They did *not* laugh.
Ivy [laughing]: And yet... here you are.
Morrie: Because I learned the most important rule: Be funny *after* you are trusted. Never to be trusted

Morrie [gesturing to his biscotti]: And never joke with food in your mouth. That's just physics.

***

Practical exercises

To practice the key ideas discussed in this chapter, work on the following three actionable exercises:

Interjection drill

Activity: During one internal or client meeting this week, identify a moment where the conversation gets either absurd (too corporate), too tense, or just plain stale. Your goal is to insert *one* dry, thoughtful, non-disruptive comment that lightens the moment, *without derailing the topic.*
Objective: Learn to deliver a subtle, well-timed, authority-raising joke in real meetings.

The alter ego exercise

Activity: For one client or internal interaction (be it a booking, a coffee run, or even a meeting intro) use a playful name, phrase, or recurring inside joke that softens your image and lowers formality. This becomes your *Johnny moment*. For example, introduce yourself on a call with a light comment: "Hi, I'm the deck wrangler and occasional truth-teller, nice to meet you all."
Objective: Build approachability and memorable presence through a crafted, lighter persona.

Deliberate self-deprecation

Activity: In a moment of introduction, presentation, or one-on-one interaction, intentionally make yourself the butt of a subtle, well-placed joke. Choose a trait or flaw that is *obvious but harmless*, keep it short and contextual, and pair it with confident body language.

Objective: Use self-deprecating humor to build psychological safety and show confident vulnerability.

Be Remembered as Brilliant

In the *Iliad*, Achilles was not just any other warrior. He was The Warrior. His rage was the stuff of nightmares, his combat skills so lethal they bordered on divine. Achilles had the level of talent that made other heroes look like extras in his personal epic. His name alone was enough to send shivers down the spines of Trojan veterans who had survived every horror of that ten-year siege, except him. Achilles was not fighting for Greece. He was not even fighting for Helen, the supposed face that *launched a thousand ships* ("Was this the face that launch'd a thousand ships / And burnt the topless towers of Ilium?" writes Christopher Marlowe in his 1592 *The Tragical History of the Life and Death of Doctor Faustus*).

Achilles fought for the only thing he truly valued: *kleos*, everlasting glory, the sort of reputation that would make people chant his name long after his corpse had rotted to dust. He wanted to be remembered not as another well-paid mercenary but as a legend.

Achilles was popular because he was strong and quick, but also a branding genius. His reputation was his sword and shield, a narrative sharpened by his fanatical desire to be the best. When Agamemnon dared to insult him by stealing Briseis, that was a direct assault on Achilles' reputation. His ego was wounded more deeply than any spear could reach.

You did not just disrespect Achilles. You insulted his very raison d'être.

So, what did he do? The most arrogant, spiteful, yet paradoxically brilliant move you could imagine: he just stopped fighting. Pulled himself out of the war and sat by his ships, fuming like a ticking bomb. His absence was felt like a missing limb. The Greek army crumbled without him, their morale shattered, their ranks reduced to chaos. Achilles had established himself as the lynchpin, and his value was so high that even his absence carried weight.

The man weaponized his own reputation. Genius.

But his obsession was far from over. He re-entered the battle not because he missed the thrill of combat, but because Hector (Troy's golden boy, its own Achilles) had slaughtered Patroclus, Achilles' closest friend, and worst of all, *dared* to wear Achilles' armor: an unforgivable crime in the world of legends. When Achilles returned, it was not to make nice with Agamemnon or play politics. It was pure rage-fueled brand management. He needed to reassert himself as the undisputed champion, the avatar of Death itself. And boy, did he deliver.

He hunted Hector like a starving wolf and, when he finally caught him, it was a public relations spectacle. Achilles killed Hector, then proceeded to mutilate him, tie his corpse to his chariot, and drag it around the walls of Troy for all to see (below an extract from A. S. Kline's translation of the *Iliad*):

> "He pierced the tendons of both feet behind from heel to ankle, and through them threaded ox-hide thongs, tying them to his chariot, leaving the corpse's head to trail along

> the ground. Then lifting the glorious armour aboard, he mounted and touched the horses with his whip, and they eagerly leapt forward. Dragged behind, Hector's corpse raised a cloud of dust, while his outspread hair flowed, black, on either side. That head, once so fine, trailed in the dirt, now Zeus allowed his enemies to mutilate his corpse on his own native soil."

A gruesome parade announcing: This is what happens when you mess with Achilles' reputation.

Reputation is a narrative

I am sure you are now wondering: why the hell did I have to read all of *that*?!

Achilles understood something most people never get: *Reputation is a narrative, and you are either controlling it or being controlled by it.* It does not matter how good you are at your job if nobody knows it, or if what they know is tainted by someone else's version of your story. Achilles' approach to reputation was extreme, sure, but the principle remains.

You cannot just hope your work will speak for itself. The world is filled with brilliant people rotting in obscurity because they never learned to make their name a sword and shield. Your reputation is not some fluffy HR metric. It's your primary asset, your anti-fragile capital, the one thing that, when wielded correctly, can carry you through the most challenging projects and the worst political storms. The story of Achilles teaches you two things: 1) Reputation is power, the kind that does not fade just because you are not in the room; and 2) if you don't protect it, if you don't actively manage it, someone else will, and they will not be nearly as charitable as you would like.

Reputation is the office's stock market. Buy low, sell high, right? Unfortunately, unlike stocks, you cannot just trade your way to a stellar reputation; you must build it.

If you are a young consultant, you are sitting on a gold mine of opportunity to shape how people perceive you: no baggage, a clean slate, a room full of people to influence and connect with, and who are ready to form an opinion about you.

First things first, always deliver quality work.

First impressions are like tattoos, hard to erase and painful to fix, and nothing tanks your name faster than sloppy deliverables. I will never forget a PowerPoint deck with typos. That's like showing up to a client meeting with mayo on your tie: the stain will go away, but the memory lingers.

You must understand that your reputation is like a multi-faceted diamond, reflecting light, or lack thereof, in several directions. One facet might be your technical prowess, another could be your team-player vibe, and yet another could be your knack for client relations. Self-promotion tends to light up only one facet (your achievements), but leaves the others in the dark. While you are gleaming in one direction, you might be causing shadows elsewhere.

Take time and do some thinking to *know your audience*. In a consulting environment, your audience is as diverse as a United Nations meeting. You have Partners eyeing revenues, managers looking at utilization rates, and teammates concerned with who is doing their fair share of the grunt work.

If you are the guy who is constantly talking up his client-revenue-increasing exploits, the Partners might love you, but what about your teammates? They might start thinking you are a self-serving mercenary. The moment you are seen as *that guy*, the one who sucks up but does not lift others, your collaboration prospects plummet.

Consider, too, the subtle nuances of corporate culture and client expectations. Some work environments value modesty and let results speak for themselves, while others celebrate victories loudly and publicly.

Always be mindful of the context.

This is why you must be strategic: selectively illuminate your successes in a way that casts a favorable glow on those around you.

Did you fix a complex bug in half the initially estimated time? Awesome. But maybe the tale you tell is not just about your technical genius. Perhaps, the story you will tell is about how the whole team came together: the functional consultant, the tester, your developer colleague, each contributing their unique skills to smash expectations.

A story like the above makes you look good, and paints you as a unifying team player. It recognizes the effort of others, which is fundamental for earning respect from your colleagues.

That is how a slight change in the narrative can lead to a significant shift in perception.

In the primordial days of digital music, when Napster roamed the earth and dial-up modems screeched like prehistoric beasts, I established myself as the Spotify of 2001 (except, unlike most of today's streaming services, I turned a profit from day one).

My business model was elegant in its simplicity: songs downloaded at geological speeds (30-40 minutes per track) were burned onto shiny discs with custom-printed (by yours truly) labels, then sold at magnificent markups to my fellow high school students. I was doing *drop-shipping* before *drop-shipping* existed. The narrative shift I preach about throughout this chapter manifested then: I was not selling pirated music, but I was providing a *white glove curation service.* You did not pay for songs: you paid for my exquisite taste and technical wizardry! The proper stroke of genius, I think, was in inventory management. Each 40-minute download represented a significant time investment in an era when tying up the family phone line could trigger domestic diplomatic incidents. The solution to that problem was to go all in on persuasion.

"You know what would pair perfectly with that *Oasis* track you requested? This *Blur* song I coincidentally already have downloaded."

"Everyone's putting *Smashing Pumpkins* on their compilation this week. Total coincidence that it's sitting right here on my hard drive."

I was selling stories about what was cool, what paired well together, and what represented good taste. My classmates were not buying tracks they could eventually download themselves, but were buying identity, convenience, and, importantly, my carefully constructed reality where certain songs were "must-haves" (specifically, the songs I had already spent half a Sunday downloading). Was it legal? Let's just say I would not have passed an audit, but it was invaluable as a laboratory for developing the persuasive skills that would later serve me in my consulting life.

I learned that people don't buy what you sell. They buy the story you tell about what you sell, so when I tell you today that narrative shapes reality, I'm not speaking theoretically: I learned it in the trenches of adolescent commerce, one painstakingly downloaded MP3 at a time.

If juggling all this makes your head spin, good: that means you are paying attention. If it were easy, every consultant would be a rock-star. You spent years memorizing industry jargon, cracking operating models, bending hyperscalers to your will, yet somehow, you think understanding *people* should be instinctive? No. In the same way you debug a system, you debug human incentives. The upside is that, once you figure that out, your brain becomes an unfair advantage, and your career shifts from slow grind to high-speed elevator.

Practice is all you need, no more simply reading about things (or, as Derek Sivers put it: "If more information were the answer, we'd all be billionaires with six-pack abs").

Self-promote (without looking like an asshole)

If you are aware of how you naturally come across, you can calibrate your actions to shape other people's perceptions better.

Understand that self-promotion is not the devil: it's a tool.

Used wisely, it can construct an enviable reputation. Used poorly, it can turn into a sledgehammer that smashes it to bits.

Chad was a colleague of mine in Australia who managed to piss off half the office in just six months: an impressive feat, really. It was like watching a slow-motion car crash, except the driver aggressively honked at pedestrians and blamed the road signs for being in his way. Chad was confident. Painfully so. He walked into the firm like he had just been personally recruited by the gods of consulting, ready to bestow his unparalleled wisdom upon us mere mortals. His favorite phrases included "Let me tell you how it is," "You are thinking about this all wrong," and, my personal favorite, "That is just not how high performers operate."

The problem turned out to be that he was not half as good as he thought he was. And his abrasive tone, combined with an ego the size of Sydney Harbour, quickly alienated everyone: senior leaders, clients, his own team, even the office receptionist, who eventually refused to transfer his calls. At first, people tried to give him the benefit of the doubt. Maybe he just needed to settle in. Perhaps he was just *direct* in that charming way some high achievers are.

Nope. Chad was just an ass. By month three, the whispers had started. By month five, his project team had unofficially renamed their group chat

"Surviving Chad" (I am not kidding!). By month six, nobody wanted to work with him: literally, nobody. Even the two analysts desperate for billable hours were suddenly *very busy* whenever Chad's name came up. Eventually, leadership had to step in. It was a *mutual decision* that Chad would "pursue other opportunities," and just like that, he was gone, leaving behind only the legend of his short but catastrophic reign. You can be brilliant, but if people cannot stand being in a room with you, it does not matter. Your reputation is not just built on results. It is built on how you make others feel while you are getting there.

Therefore, please go ahead and be your PR agency, but be tactful. Know which stories to pitch, to whom, and when.

Find a mentor or a more experienced colleague and let them amplify your achievements. When your boss says, "Have you seen the work that the new guy did on the X project? Awe-inspiring stuff," their words carry weight. It is better than a LinkedIn post because you don't have to humiliate yourself with a humblebrag. Think of it as a celebrity endorsement, only it's free, and you don't even have to ask for it.

Speaking of mentors, get close to someone who's got clout but also aligns with your work ethic and style. You don't want to be stuck with an Andrew who lacks empathy and only looks out for himself!

Try to understand who is on the rise in your leadership team and spend time with that person. They are doing well because they are good at their job and can control the delicate balance between acquiring domain knowledge, building client relationships, and exercising their soft skills within the firm with mastery. Proximity equals osmosis: soak up what you can.

I have put myself in this situation several times throughout my career. In fact, I can definitely link any big step during my professional journey to an incredible mentor who pushed me toward achieving milestones I didn't think I could.

In this book, I have referred often to my time in Hong Kong because that's the one that sticks the most with people, but did I ever mention the time an ex-colleague, ten years my senior, became MD of a boutique consultancy and hired me with a *50% salary bump*?

Ah, now I have your attention.

When I returned to Europe from Asia, I was feeling a little itchy. I took some time off to rest and recalibrate, and think through the type of professional challenges I wanted to take on in the coming years. After spending some days on the coast of Southern Italy, closer to home and under the care of my parents, I felt energized and ready to fuel the next leg of my career.

By then, I had worked for a massive firm and then a mid-sized company, but I had never tested myself in a smaller enterprise. I felt that, coming on the back of a successful and tiresome international project, was a good time to switch organizations and work toward more control and seniority.

That's when I reached out to Rich.

Rich was this Irish fella I had met a few years earlier when he and I were being inducted into a new firm. It was both our first day, and despite the difference in age, we hit it off straight away (mostly bonding over a shared hatred of British weather and the Tube.)

Rich was the kind of guy who could walk into a room and have the entire place laughing within minutes. Not in a forced, attention-seeking way: just effortless charisma. He had a way with words, a sharp wit that could cut through the dullest meeting like a hot knife through butter. If you were stuck in a workshop where the air had gone stale from corporate jargon, all it took was one perfectly timed remark from Rich to have everyone stifling laughter behind their notepads.

He was also brilliant, with a rare mix of charm and intellect. Some consultants can talk a good game but fumble when it comes to actual insight. Rich was not one of them. He had this uncanny ability to ask the one question that made the entire room pause. He was casual about it: "Well, have we thought about ABC?" And suddenly, you realized that no, nobody had thought about ABC, and now the entire strategy needed a rethink. It was annoying in the best possible way.

We briefly worked together on a project, and I made it my mission to absorb as much as I could from him. When we shared meeting spaces and long hours grinding numbers, I tried to make a good impression, but honestly, it was hard not to. He just liked me. We clicked. He could see I was sharp and driven, and I could see he was someone worth learning from.

Even after we stopped working in the same project team, our catching up continued to happen (unsurprisingly) over beer and pub food. Rich was a terrible influence, because he could easily convince you to stay for "just one more" at the pub and, before you knew it, the bartender was announcing last call and you were debating whether a 2 am *plastic-y pizza* in Leicester Square was a good idea (it always was). We would trade war stories from the firm between bites of questionable Shepherd's pies that London pubs found suitable to serve. I would update him on whatever projects I was wrestling with and, in return, he would give me gold-tier career advice, usually delivered between sips of Guinness, with his trademark smirk.

And it was not all work-bro talk. Rich had two kids whom he absolutely adored. He never did the whole *workaholic dad* routine; you could tell he was properly invested in their lives. He would tell me stories about them with the pride that made it clear that, for all his consulting brilliance, those two were his real legacy.

But let's be honest: most of our conversations devolved into merciless football banter. Rich was a die-hard Manchester United fan, and I, of course, had my own allegiances. We would talk so much shit about each other's teams that sometimes bystanders at the pub genuinely thought we were about to fight. We never did, of course. Our friendship was built to withstand the worst of Premier League seasons. Rich was, and still is, one of my absolute favorite people. Brilliant, hilarious, and just a proper, solid guy. I love him to bits, and if you ever get the chance to have a pint with him, do not pass it up.

My star in that consulting firm was rising, and even though we were in different departments, I made it a point to put my minor achievements and ambitions into orbit so that influential people like Rich could take notice. I already told you: words travel fast in our world and gravitate to potential opportunities.

By the time I had completed my assignment in Hong Kong, Rich had become the Managing Director of a rising consulting firm in the UK, and we had kept talking. When I decided to scout for a potential pivot to a smaller firm, he was my first call. All I had to ask him was: "How's the outlook? Do you think somebody like me could be helpful?"

If he had not heard good things around me in our circle, our little corporate universe, I am sure the conversation would have gone very differently.

Instead, all it took was a short discussion over beers at *The George* in London (time truly is a flat circle) followed by a meeting with the Group CEO, which led to a job offer: a job offer with an improved title and a hike of 50% to my compensation package.

Why people should enjoy working with you

Networking intelligently and cultivating a positive reputation are the most catalyzing things you can do in your career.

Whenever you have the chance, think about social capital. Let's say you are savvy with data analytics, or you are the go-to person for change management. Offer those skills to colleagues, even if it's not directly related to your project. The point is to be seen as resourceful and collaborative, not just competent.

Your reputation is your brand, a composite of the impressions you have made. Just like any brand, it requires some astute management.

Results are vital to a robust reputation: they are your report card. Think of results as the *product features* of your brand. If you can make the company more money, or save time, or innovate solutions, people will naturally think highly of you. But that's just table stakes in consulting.

There is also *perception*, and that's the silent hill where many bright young consultants usually stumble. They believe that stellar results automatically generate an excellent reputation.

Not so fast.

I have seen consultants who delivered incredible results but were still labeled as difficult or toxic. Why? Because they ignored the *user experience* of working with them. In the same way a product is not just about features but about how it makes the user feel, your reputation is not just about what you do but about how you make others feel when you do it.

Are you respectful? Do you listen? Are you approachable? These soft skills influence the perception others have of you.

The challenges of perception are followed by alignment. In a corporate context, alignment refers to how well you jive with the company's goals, culture, and existing dynamics. You could be a lone wolf who delivers excellent results, but if you are not in sync with the broader objectives of the firm or if you clash with the team, you will hit the ceiling eventually, career-wise. Companies in general, and consulting firms specifically, want team players who amplify everyone else's efforts.

And now, for the part everyone *hates* to admit they need to do: politicking.

"Oh, but I just want my work to speak for itself." Good luck: you might as well be waiting for the tooth fairy to negotiate your bonus. The world does not work that way. Nobody likes a kiss-up, but nobody likes a clueless idealist either, especially one who believes meritocracy is some divine law of physics. The truth is, your organization is likely a messy, often irrational, sometimes ego-driven ecosystem where influence trumps raw talent. Those who understand this do not "game the system" but simply refuse to be blind to its reality. Politics exists in *every* human system. Even monasteries have power struggles over who gets the best saffron robe.

The key is not to sell your soul, but to learn the rules and play them with integrity:

- Who really calls the shots? (Hint: it is often *not* the person with the biggest title, but the one with the biggest sway.)
- What do they care about? (Spoiler: Not your technical brilliance, but how your work makes them look better.)
- How do you get on their radar, without looking desperate? (Think chess, not checkers.)

Politicking is not about faking enthusiasm for bad ideas or throwing colleagues under the bus. It is about strategic alignment and moving in a way that feels authentic to you. Do not betray yourself: just ensure you are *in* the room when the big decisions happen.

Like one of those sandcastles that my daughter loves to build at Avoca Beach in the Central Coast of New South Wales *downunder*, reputation does not sit there untouched but is always at risk of erosion. All it takes is one strong wave of office gossip, misunderstandings, a single lousy impression, and years of good work are gone. If you want to build something that *lasts,* you need to stop treating reputation as an afterthought, but must manage it like you would an investment portfolio: actively, with a long-term view. Every project, every conversation, every meeting is the grain of sand you should shape intentionally to build a fortress that can weather even the pettiest political hurricanes.

Roll up your sleeves, grab your proverbial pail and shovel, and start laying bricks to create your impregnable reputation.

***

—

Vignette

Morrie and Ivy are on a flight to a client site. Ivy keeps fiddling with her seatbelt like she is defusing a bomb.

Ivy: I am going to screw this up. I keep running through everything. I do *not* want to look sloppy.
Morrie [without looking up from his coffee]: Good. Sloppy consultants are roadkill.
Ivy: [sighs] I have so many people to meet, learn from, impress... I might actually puke. I want them to like me so badly.
Morrie [finally looks at her]: You do not need to be liked. You need to be *respected*. Big difference. Read the room like a stand-up comic. And remember that bombing in front of a sleep-deprived, Xanax-fueled C-suite is way uglier than bombing at a bad comedy club.
Ivy [panicking]: You think I am going to bomb?
Morrie [smirking]: No. I think you are overthinking. You are the new sheriff in town. Walk in like you own the damn badge.
Ivy [hesitant]: But what if I come off like an arrogant asshole?
Morrie: You will, if you make it all about you. Shine the light in all directions, not just on yourself. That is how you lead without losing the room.
Ivy [grinning]: You sound like Gandalf having a corporate meltdown.
Morrie [deadpan]: Good. Gandalf survived two wars and a Balrog. You can survive a client meeting.

***

Practical exercises

To practice the key ideas discussed in this chapter, work on the following three actionable exercises:

Self-assessment and feedback
Activity: Conduct a thorough self-assessment of your reputation in the firm. Identify your strengths, areas for improvement, and how you believe others perceive you. Then, seek feedback from colleagues, mentors, and supervisors on your performance, interpersonal skills, and areas for improvement.
Objective: To gain a clear and accurate understanding of how others perceive you, and identify specific areas for improvement. This will provide a solid foundation for strategically enhancing your reputation.

Practice consistent quality
Activity: Choose a current project and commit to delivering it with the highest quality possible. Focus on details, ensure it is error-free, and exceed your and team's expectations. Document your process, including the extra steps you took, and reflect on team and client feedback.
Objective: To establish a habit of delivering high-quality work consistently. This exercise aims to reinforce the importance of quality in building a strong reputation, and to demonstrate how exceptional deliverables can positively impact others' perceptions of you.

Strategic self-promotion
Activity: Identify a recent success to share with your team and leadership, highlighting both your and your colleagues' contributions. Craft a nar-

rative emphasizing teamwork, and share it during a team meeting or in a project update email.

Objective: To practice the art of strategic self-promotion that enhances your reputation while recognizing and uplifting others. This exercise aims to teach you how to communicate your achievements in a way that generates positive perceptions and strengthens team cohesion.

The Wise Grow What Others Long For

Diocletian, if you have never heard of him, was the Roman emperor who effectively said, "I'm done with your nonsense," then split the entire Empire into manageable chunks (the *Tetrarchy*), so he could enjoy fewer migraines from would-be usurpers. That was the easy part.

He then performed a feat so miraculous that modern corporate suits cannot quite believe it: he voluntarily stepped down, a CEO so fed up with the boardroom drama that he packed his stuff and headed to the countryside in the ancient Roman city of Salona, located in modern-day Split, Croatia, to grow vegetables (cabbages, specifically).

The man who once bossed around legions and dictated the fate of millions found more satisfaction in the knotted leaves of humble *Brassica oleracea* than in the sycophantic praise of the Senate. His pals could not process this and kept begging him to return to power after his abdication, to which he famously replied: *"Utinam Salonae possetis visere olera nostris manibus instituta, profecto numquam istud temptandum iudicaretis."*

Translated, this means: "If you could see at Salona the cabbages raised by our hands, you surely would never judge that a temptation." In other words, dear senators, watch me cultivate something real for once.

Now, put this in perspective: Diocletian orchestrates possibly the most prominent corporate re-org in ancient history, then, right when everyone thinks he will cling to the power seat forever (like the average modern executive or typical politician who is glued to the corner office until forcibly carried out), he opts out. A cynic might say he wanted to escape future scandals or hedge himself against inevitable political collapse. Still, I find it more meaningful to see it as a quest for *personal antifragility*: better to be a cabbage grower than a weak figurehead in a disintegrating empire.

It is shocking how so many *leaders* never figure out this simple equation. They remain drunk on titles and ceremonials, like the guy who confuses a *VP of Something Corporate* plaque with actual knowledge or skill. Meanwhile, Diocletian discovered the stoic joy of watering soil with his sweat, ironically proving far more rewarding than reigning over sweaty Roman politicians. He found contentment in manual labor, in the tangible gratification of nurturing green shoots. Doesn't that remind you of the frustration so many in business feel once they realize that *driving shareholder value* might be a giant rhetorical treadmill?

We measure nonsense, then wonder why we are never satisfied. The moral seems simple: when you find meaning in what you do, not from external applause, but from the internal "I built this, I grew that, I made a small dent in the world," you are forging your own path. Diocletian, in all his contrarian glory, delivered the ultimate mic-drop by picking a garden over a kingdom.

If that doesn't make you question your next chase for corporate confetti, I don't know what will.

Consulting is the ultimate seduction game for ambitious professionals. The six-figure salaries, the business-class flights, the steak dinners, the illusion of corporate power, the idea that you are the puppet master pulling the strings of multinational empires.

It's a siren call so enticing that makes Odysseus' voyage sound like a stroll through a suburban mall.

But if all you are chasing is materialistic gain, you are on a collision course with disappointment, because external rewards, as enticing as they are, are the junk food of motivation. Tastes fantastic, gives you a sugar rush, and then leaves you feeling hollow, and, worst of all, addicted.

The problem is not the rewards themselves. There is nothing wrong with a hefty bonus or the thrill of your name being dropped with admiration at a Partner's dinner party. These are quick dopamine hits that even get you some credibility in the right circles, but if these things become your North Star, your consulting career will end up about as memorable as the last season of a dying Netflix series.

Let's talk about hedonic adaptation, the psychological equivalent of running on a treadmill you thought was an escalator. You get the salary bump, the praise, the promotion, and it feels like you just won the lottery. You are high on achievement for a couple of weeks, maybe even a couple of months. Then the joy deflates like an undercooked soufflé. What thrilled you yesterday becomes your new baseline today, and your new baseline starts to feel like a prison by tomorrow. It's a never-ending race, and instead of chasing actual fulfillment, you are chasing a corporate high (except your drug is not crack, it's perks, prestige, and the illusion of permanence).

The worst part of it all is that you are a consultant, you work in a performance-driven industry where metrics rule the land. As we discussed earlier, all the shiny little metrics your firm cares about are the golden ticket to external validation. When you hit them, they throw you a few bones: bonuses, promotions, and a healthy pat on the back.

But what happens when the numbers don't align? When the project go south for reasons that have nothing to do with you? I have seen bright, ambitious consultants melt down like over-pressurized kettles when things go sideways. Some throw tantrums, others spiral into self-doubt, jealousy, or both. It's an ugly sight.

That's the moment you realize that external rewards are fair-weather friends. They are like parasitic acquaintances who party with you when the *Prosecco* flows and vanish when the lights go out. They keep you grinding at unsustainable levels until your nervous system files a formal complaint. That's where most consultants stumble: they never realize that the only way to win the game is to stop playing it.

The alternative is finding your intrinsic motivation, the slow-burning, self-replenishing fuel that makes the journey itself the reward, the thing that keeps you going even when the external accolades dry up. It's the joy of solving a problem so tricky it makes your head hurt, but you still love the challenge. It's the satisfaction of seeing a client's sinking ship stabilize because of your work. It's finding pride in the craft itself.

Consulting is a marathon run at a sprinter's pace. There will be sleepless nights, demanding clients, internal politics, and pressure so intense it feels like someone's holding your head underwater. If you don't have a robust *why* fueled by intrinsic motivation, your *how* will be a stress-laden mess, and you will burn out faster than a firecracker thrown into a blast furnace.

I have some good news. Intrinsic motivation is like a fine *Chianti*: it gets better over time, if you nurture it. Finding what truly drives you is not a one-off event but a constant process of introspection, evolution, and recalibration. What motivates you today might not work five years from now, and that's fine. Your internal compass will drift, but you will stay on course as long as you keep finetuning it. This internal exercise of reflection is not about rejecting external rewards. It's about making sure they are just the side dishes, not the main course. The thrill of the game, the joy of getting better at your craft, the satisfaction of making a real impact: those are the metrics that matter, the Diocletian's cabbages of your career, the things you build for yourself, that no title, bonus, or fancy dinner can replace.

Once you embrace your intrinsic motivation, you can keep building while others burn out.

The dirty little secret of staying motivated in consulting

Your task is not purely *finding your passion*, that's motivational poster fluff. You must dig deep and reverse-engineer what genuinely fuels you, not what looks good on a LinkedIn profile.

Take a weekend off. That's right, an entire weekend. Not the "I'll just check emails between Netflix episodes" kind. The real deal. Disconnect from your devices, find a quiet spot, and, without distractions, run a full diagnostic scan on yourself. Just you, your thoughts, and maybe a double espresso if you are feeling particularly existential.

Start with the basics: What do you actually enjoy doing? I'm not talking about vague stuff like *solving problems* or *being a team player.* That's brochure-speak. Go deeper. Why do you like solving problems? Is it the dopamine hit of unraveling complexity? The analytical high of turning data spaghetti into something that makes sense? Is it the human element, understanding what makes people and businesses tick, and finding ways to make them tick better?

Get granular. Brutally granular. You can't bullshit yourself here. Don't lull yourself into complacency and then slowly poison your career.

Take whatever you have unearthed, and map it to your actual job. Say you love the analytical rigor of breaking down complex systems. Great. You need to hunt down projects that let you flex those muscles actively. Talk to your manager. Make it known. Find the intersection where your passion and your professional responsibilities overlap.

Maybe your real drive comes from mentorship, connecting with people, and guiding them toward growth. Perfect. You do not have to be some gray-haired senior executive to make that work: the title is irrelevant. The will is what counts here. Offer to guide the junior analyst who stutters during presentations like he's reading the whole ingredients list printed on a box of Oreos. Teach the new intern a few killer Excel hacks, how to properly format a Word doc or some critical PowerPoint shortcuts. Create value for others while sharpening your skills. It's called mutually beneficial work, and it's addictive. It also makes the hellish hours worth something.

When the projects pile up, when the stress level hits DEFCON 1 and everything around you is falling apart, your intrinsic motivators are most at risk. Give yourself constant reminders. Write them down and revisit them regularly, not because you are some self-help junkie, but because clarity fades over time, and the more you grind, the more you forget why you are even grinding. It does not matter if the reminders are physical or digital. It could be a sticky note on your monitor, a journal entry, or a Notion page you update every week, but make sure those motivators are always in your line of sight.

Ask yourself:

- Did this week's work make me feel more aligned with what I enjoy doing?

- Am I feeling engaged, or am I just going through the motions?
- What must I change to keep my intrinsic motivators alive and kicking?

Use the answers to create your own personal *dashboard* of fulfillment. Your motivations will evolve over time: as you gain experience, face new challenges, or grow older and crankier, your motivators will change. It's all good. That's normal. It's a feature, not a bug, simply just make sure you are recalibrating your internal compass as you go along.

Understanding and aligning with your intrinsic motivation is not a luxury; it is not the cherry on top of your consulting career. It's the bloody foundation! Without it, everything else is a house of cards waiting for a mild breeze to knock it down.

I can guarantee this is not some *all feel-good* nonsense: let me tell you a secret about what has kept me in this people-facing, client-serving, globe-trotting circus for two damn decades.

I indeed have had days where I wanted to torch my laptop and walk away, but even when I questioned my sanity and fought off existential dread, I kept coming back. Why? Because I had something beyond money and promotions guiding me. It was the joy of improving myself at *appreciating skills* that got better over time. Skills like communication, persuasion, negotiation, empathy, and yes, connecting with people. The *soft* skills that are hard as hell to master but pay off like compound interest once you get them right. I love learning, and I find genuine fulfillment in helping others grow, from guiding clueless interns, to turning smart colleagues into superstars, to understanding clients' unstated needs before *they* even know what they want.

The intangible, people-driven side of consulting is what makes this madness worthwhile. The only real competitive advantage you will ever have in this relentless, high-performance landscape is this: Loving what you do, even when it makes you want to pull your hair out (I play the game on easy mode because I'm bald).

My Intrinsic Motivator

Consulting is a people business.

You will teach people.

You will report to people.

You will work with people.

You will argue with people.

You will buy and sell from and to people.

You will co-design new concepts with people.

You will share and explore ideas with people.

You will receive feedback from people.

You will give feedback to people.

You will collaborate with people.

You will reconcile with people.

You will learn from people.

At its core, consulting is about positively influencing the key decision-makers (i.e., other people) in an organization to drive change. The technical skills are secondary to connecting with these people, winning them over through empathy and reason, and inspiring a shared sense of purpose.

Just about anything you will do in your consulting profession will have to do with people, one way or the other.

Everything associated with the work you do might differ depending on the time or team, but the focus on influencing people will be the only constant.

For example, you might change your niche. Your interests will be different over time. Technology will evolve and progress.

Twenty years ago, I operated a solo business that helped small enterprises run their IT operations.

Fifteen years ago, I worked as a systems integrator for large organizations that dealt with their finance systems.

Ten years ago, I was a specialist in core financial services business and technology re-engineering.

Five years ago, I built a management consulting practice for a tech giant starting from scratch.

A lot has changed over 20 years.

The only constant? I have to handle and work with *people* to achieve professional objectives.

As an innovator and architect, Richard Buckminster Fuller highlighted the following: "There is nothing in a caterpillar that tells you it's going to be a butterfly."

Likewise, the industries, technologies, and techniques consultants apply will inevitably change unpredictably throughout a career, and we won't know how exactly. For example, nobody truly can predict what AI will make of the business world in ten years (beware of the gurus who tell you otherwise). However, consultants build transferable skills to evolve alongside shifting environments by focusing on timeless truths of what makes people, teams, and organizations tick. Seek first to understand the people, and the technical problems and solutions will come into focus.

Early on, I was like everyone else. My obsession was mastering *the current thing*. I wanted to be the best damn SAP finance systems expert on the planet. And you know what? I probably was one of the best damn SAP finance systems experts on the planet. But it meant nothing.

At some point in my career, I realized that if I wanted to make the step and become more than just the great guy who fixes things, I had to expand my competence from technology and business to human interactions.

I understood that how we relate to people becomes more important than how good we are at a particular technology, drawing data on charts, manipulating Excel, or developing my client's new technology strategy. The most brilliant solution will flounder without a genuine understanding of, and connection with, the people impacted. To become an irresistible consultant, I had to focus on forging solid ties and understanding unspoken needs, earning permission to drive change in a way the tactical expert never can.

I realized, for example, that learning and practicing persuasion, negotiations, conflict management, and effective communication would pay dividends for far longer than learning the next trick on SAP or the next business framework.

The former are *appreciating skills* and the latter depreciate with time.

Years ago, I was leading a project where my team and I were hitting every milestone. We were blowing them to smithereens, finishing tasks days (sometimes weeks) ahead of schedule. We were high-fiving each other, living under the grand delusion that everyone would be thrilled. The other consulting firm on the project, more prominent than us and cozier with the CIO, was unhappy that they had to nurse bruised egos because our efficiency made them look slow. Instead of everyone singing *Kumbaya*, we effectively set off a silent turf war. I was young, unseasoned, and convinced that if the work was flawless, the politics didn't matter (it turns out that the Rolling Stones were right: "You can't always get what you want"). The CIO did not like the friction. From his perspective, *synergy* (that dreaded word) was a must.

Meanwhile, I went all-out and perhaps stepped on a few toes (more, I was setting the entire dance floor on fire), almost reveling in a confrontation. I assumed results were king, that I was indispensable. And that's when the CIO swiftly reminded me that no one is indispensable. Next thing I know, I'm the one getting thrown under the bus, courtesy of a phone call that started with, "We appreciate all you have done, but..." In that glorious fiasco, I discovered there is a reason it's called *people* business. All the technical wizardry in the world won't save you if you manage to make powerful allies look bad or feel bad. You can be the best chess player in the club, but if the game suddenly switches to poker and you don't know how to bluff, you are out of chips. After that debacle, I doubled down on negotiation skills, conflict management, and persuasion, the *soft skills* that are *alpha skills* in consulting.

I always found it ironic: what people typically call *soft skills* are all but soft! They generally are harder (to learn and apply) than those that people commonly refer to as hard skills. If you don't believe me, just think of that colleague who is a whiz at whatever he does, but falls apart in a simple conversation, and cannot explain their job to a human without resorting to jargon and hand-waving. I bet it didn't take you long to picture someone, did it?

Billionaire investor Warren Buffett attributes almost all of his success to having strong communication and people skills rather than innate technical genius. He says: "I'm not the smartest guy in the world by any measure... But I can assemble people who are smarter than I and work well with them."

The wisdom to recognize individual limitations and unite complementary minds lies at the heart of consulting excellence. Cultivate relationship talents and intuition to make people understand your ideas and buy into them.

Improving your transferable meta-skills

I learned to find joy in improving at all those transferable, appreciating meta-skills, the ones that grow more valuable as time and technology march forward and let you pivot when the industry does its next Great Schism.

I learned to love learning and practicing how to improve my communication, how to improve my writing, and speaking, how to become a more effective negotiator (for myself and the firms I worked for), how to enhance my quick learning abilities (so that I can rapidly pivot as everything around me changes).

My day-to-day consulting work is an opportunity to practice and get better.

Learning to master the social game is a contrarian bet. The market overvalues technical skills and undervalues relational mastery, so the long-term value must be in betting against the herd, going long on the skills others neglect. My intrinsic motivation is built on this very insight: *Consistently improving at my appreciating skills while staying relevant in the value I provide to my team and clients as everything changes around us.*

The idea is to build a sustainable competitive advantage, a moat around your career that protects you against the inevitable disruptions, re-organizations, and market shifts that leave the technical-only guys crying into their overpriced ergonomic chairs.

The more you invest in appreciating skills, the more you begin to shape your luck. You become the guy who connects the dots nobody else sees, the consultant who understands what truly matters to clients and colleagues, even when they cannot clearly articulate it themselves. You make yourself valuable, not because you are just a technical savant, but because you are a connector of people, ideas, and opportunities.

This process never stops.

The longer I stay in the game, the more valuable these skills become. Every tough conversation I navigate, every junior consultant I mentor, every crisis I help defuse, all add to my arsenal. It's a game of compound interest, and the returns are exponential. The irony is that most consultants never get this. They are too busy chasing the latest framework, the hottest tech trend, the new buzzword to slap on their LinkedIn profiles (remember all those *blockchain evangelists*?). They are updating their résumés with tactical garbage, while I'm building a foundation that cannot be replaced by the next shiny thing or "AI".

It's a simple equation, really:

- Technical skills = Rent. They give you temporary value, and you must keep paying to stay relevant.

- Appreciating skills = Equity. They grow in value and give you leverage that no one can take away.

This realization is why I am still in this business after two decades, and why my passion for consulting keeps burning while others burn out. I find joy in becoming better, guiding others along their journeys, and staying sharp enough to learn from them as much as they learn from me.

***

Vignette

Morrie is switching focus between his laptop and a report. A frown has taken over his usual jolly face. Ivy walks in like he usually does without knocking.

Ivy: Morrie. I got you some lunch. You need to eat, man. I have never seen you consumed by work.
Morrie: Ah. Yes, thanks, Ivy. Just one of those days. This is not a sustainable way of doing things. But some days it needs to be done.
Ivy: How long has it been? 20 years, and you still care enough. Not many promotions left for you; you know that, right?
Morrie: If I had cared about promotions or bonuses, I would have climbed this hill. I think I would have fallen off in the first few steps.
Ivy: You really like staring at projections and repetitive slides? If I had the courage, I would be a stand-up comic.
Morrie: Ivy, Ivy. C'mon. I am here 'cause I genuinely love meeting people and solving problems for them, and now mentoring smart young people like you.
Ivy: But hand to heart, if it were not for the paycheck and prestige? That's true, right?
Morrie [smirking]: Hand to heart. I am still upset that my punk rock drummer career never worked. In many ways, my life is still similar to that of a rock star.
Ivy: The long hours, constant traveling, decent money, and mild addictions. True, you are a rockstar, in a way.
Morrie: And you are a stand-up comic, in a way.

***

Practical exercises

To practice the key ideas discussed in this chapter, work on the following three actionable exercises:

Deep-dive into self-reflection
Activity: Dedicate a weekend to introspection. Reflect deeply on what drives you, considering questions like:
- What work activities satisfy me most?
- Why do they bring me joy?
- What aspects are fulfilling beyond rewards?
Journal your thoughts, aiming to uncover underlying motivations.
Objective: To uncover your intrinsic motivators and to gain a deeper understanding of what drives you beyond external rewards. This exercise aims to help you align your daily activities and long-term goals with these intrinsic motivations for a more fulfilling career.

Aligning passions with professional roles
Activity: Based on your findings from the exercise above, identify tasks in your role that match your intrinsic motivations. Seek complex analytical tasks if you enjoy problem-solving, or mentor junior consultants if mentorship excites you. Discuss your interests with your manager to find aligned opportunities.
Objective: To synchronize your professional responsibilities with your intrinsic passions, ensuring that your daily work contributes to your internal sense of fulfillment and satisfaction.

Establishing intrinsic goals and tracking progress

Activity: Set actionable goals focused on personal growth, such as improving communication by presenting and getting feedback or developing novel expertise in areas that excite you. Track progress in a journal or digital document, regularly reflecting and adjusting based on activities that align with your inherent motivations.

Objective: To establish and pursue intrinsic goals that promote personal growth and satisfaction. Tracking progress and reflecting regularly ensures you stay aligned with your internal motivations and adapt as they evolve.

TAKE THE SHORTCUT THAT MAKES THE ROAD LONGER

Johann Wolfgang von Goethe was 18th-century Germany's literary rock star, a polymath who dabbled in poetry, science, and just about everything else that caught his restless mind. I'm pretty convinced Germany's last good decision (after the 1516 *Reinheitsgebot*, their beer purity law) was letting Goethe run free with a quill. These days, people read his works to feel cultured, to appear sophisticated, maybe even to pick up a dash of that creative genius by osmosis, but Goethe's masterpiece, *Faust*, is less about refinement and more about humanity's eternal soft spot: the willingness to gamble our soul (or at least our integrity) for a shortcut to what we want right now.

Faust, the character, is a brilliant scholar who is bored out of his skull with knowledge. One ill-advised decision later, he is literally signing a contract with the devil and surrendering his future for immediate gratification. Swap out the parchment and demon for a modern corporate contract and a bullish CFO, and you see the parallels.

A *Mephistopheles* always whispers, "Hey, just sign here, and all your problems disappear." It sounds good until the Faustian price tag shows up at your door. Goethe's point stands in any era: the moment you decide to cross that ethical line, whether it's cooking the books or promising performance results you know you cannot deliver, you are bartering away something infinitely more valuable than a line item on a balance sheet. You cannot firewall off one lie from the rest of your life; compromise trickles through everything like ink in water.

Faust ends up neck-deep in regret, as will any consultant who thinks cheating the scoreboard is a brilliant strategy. The devil always comes to collect and is never in the mood to negotiate a discount.

I chose this subject as our last chapter (well, excluding the *bonus* one coming next) because it encompasses everything we have been talking about till now. The ability to navigate ethical gray areas, especially under pressure, separates the wheat from the chaff.

This is not about following company guidelines or professional codes of conduct.

It's about defining your guardrails: your *Consultant's Dharma.*

Carefully define your Dharma

Dharma is one of those deep, sprawling concepts in Indian philosophy, rooted in Hinduism but woven into Buddhism, Jainism, and Sikhism, that doesn't suffer a neat one-word translation into any Western language. Think of it as the guiding moral current, the built-in ethical compass that tells you which way is *right living* versus the slippery slope that leads to chaos.

For our purposes here, consider Dharma to be your ethical backbone as a consultant: the set of lines you simply will not cross, even if the client waves all the gold in Fort Knox under your nose, or, if you are a Satoshi Nakamoto fan, all the Bitcoin on Microstrategy's balance sheet. Dharma is where your *I refuse to compromise* stance comes from, the unshakable foundation of principles that keeps your conscience intact no matter what storms the job throws at you.

Allow me to take a little detour into game theory, a subject where people typically put on their intellectual monocles, but which, if you have the right mindset, can reveal something very practical. Here is a classic story from my favorite mathematical discipline: the *Stag Hunt.*

Imagine two hunters in the wild. They can either go after a stag or a rabbit. The stag is a big, juicy prize, but you need both hunters to succeed. If one of them backs out and goes after the rabbit, they both end up with nothing; if they both go for the stag, they eat well. The catch is that if one hunter is greedy or shortsighted and runs off to grab the rabbit, everyone loses.

In the game of life, your ethical choices are like those two hunters deciding whether to go for the stag or the rabbit. When you stick to your principles, when you do not compromise your values for a quick win, you are hunting the stag. Such an approach requires trust, and trust is built over time, with people who share your values. You need a partner who, like you, is in it for the long game, and won't ditch you for a quick rabbit. When you live by your *Dharma*, you start attracting people who also want *stags*. On the flip side, when you cut corners or manipulate your way into results, you are just grabbing that rabbit, and everyone around you is either doing the same or worse. You are surrounded by opportunists who are playing short-term games, and good luck getting anything meaningful done in that environment.

When you think in decades, the more ethical you are, the better people you attract.

Let me take you back to an incident early in my career when I was working in London, dealing with a well known local bank as my client.

As often happens in these situations, big bucks were on the line as we worked on building a business case for a multi-million-pound initiative. A Senior Manager, let's call him Jack, leaned in during a meeting and suggested we *nudge* some numbers to make it easier for our clients to accept certain conclusions we wanted to drive home.

Jack was a tall man in his 50s, with reddish hair that always looked slightly unkempt and a complexion so pale, akin to a blank Word document, that it seemed untouched by sunlight. There was something elusive about him; you could never quite read him. He was polite and professional but distant, as if every interaction was a careful performance. Nobody knew much about his personal life, and perhaps that was by design. His stiff demeanor, measured words, and the way he carried himself in meetings felt like a shield, a way to keep people from seeing whatever insecurities lurked beneath the surface. Jack was not an evil guy, but pressure does funny things to people, even those whose blood type is apparently "conditional formatting." But the moment you compromise on ethics, you set off a chain reaction that is hard to stop.

This is not just about you. Your choices ripple outward: to your team, your clients, even the industry at large.

I was young, and the request unsettled me. It was not a blatant order, just a quiet ask, the kind that slips into a conversation almost unnoticed. But I noticed. And I knew that once you take that first step over the line, even a small one, it becomes easier to justify the next. So I pushed back, but carefully. Instead of turning it into a confrontation, I made it a conversation. I asked questions. I reframed the issue. I steered us toward the bigger picture (turns out nudging works both ways).

We had spent six relentless weeks trying to build a solid case, peeling back layers of the client's business, hoping to find the numbers that would hold up under scrutiny. Unfortunately, everywhere we looked, we hit a wall. The data did not support the story we wanted to tell, and the client executives wanted those numbers to work just as badly as we did.

It is easy to convince yourself that tweaking a number here or smoothing an assumption there is just part of the game. After all, the goal is to get the *right* decision made. And yet, numbers are not just numbers. They do not sit in isolation. They shape the story, dictate the logic, become the foundation for actions with real consequences. A flawed premise, dressed up as truth, does not merely lead to bad decisions, but erodes trust. And once trust is gone, you are left with nothing.

We chose the more arduous path: no shortcuts or embellishments. We went back, combed through the data again, and told the story as it was, not as we wished it to be. The project still succeeded (!), not because we bent reality to fit our needs, but because we found a way to make an honest case that stood on its own.

More than that, I walked away with something far more valuable than a temporary win. I left that engagement knowing I had done right by myself, my team, and the principles defining real credibility in this business.

Integrity is the foundation of everything that lasts.

Cultivate Phronesis

Navigating this ethical labyrinth requires emotional intelligence and situational awareness. You need to cultivate what the ancient Greeks called *phronesis*.

Phronesis is usually translated as "practical wisdom" or "prudence," it is one of the key virtues in Aristotle's *Nicomachean Ethics*. While other forms of knowledge, like *episteme* (scientific or theoretical knowledge) and *techne* (craftsmanship or technical skill), are essential, *phronesis* is what enables us to apply them in real-world situations. It is the ability to discern the right course of action when faced with uncertainty, balancing principle with pragmatism.

In *Nicomachean Ethics*, Aristotle argues that the highest aim of human life is *eudaimonia*, a fancy Greek word often translated as "flourishing" or "the good life." Despite being born in the heart of today's European Union, Aristotle was not one of those modern European bureaucrats who thinks everything can be mapped out neatly in a policy manual. He thought that achieving *eudaimonia* is not about blindly following rules; it requires virtue, and virtue itself is a habit, a cultivated disposition to act rightly. *Phronesis* is central to this because ethical decisions are rarely black and white. Unlike mathematical truths, moral judgments depend on context, relationships, and a nuanced understanding of consequences.

Aristotle contrasts *phronesis* with *sophia* (theoretical wisdom), which is concerned with abstract truth and contemplation. *Sophia* helps us grasp eternal principles, which is nice if you live in front of a Mediterranean beach and spend your day drinking spritz while pondering the eternal nature of triangles, but not so helpful when your client just demanded impossible results by yesterday. *Phronesis,* on the other hand, allows us to navigate the messy, imperfect realities of life, where decisions must be made under pressure, with incomplete information, and often in morally ambiguous situations. You have to know what is right and also have the judgment and courage to act on it.

This distinction matters because consulting is not a game of perfect information. You will often find yourself in situations where no textbook answer exists, where data is incomplete, client expectations, office politics, and personal integrity pull in different directions. In moments like these, it is *phronesis*, not rigid adherence to formulas or methodologies, that determines the right course of action. It allows you to balance competing interests, push back when necessary, and ultimately make decisions that stand the test of time.

Assume that you just started a new project with a new client.

Your *episteme* might tell you the textbook way to design a new operating model for the business. Your *techne* will guide you through the software and models you need to make these improvements. But it's your *phronesis* that enables you to understand the nuances of this particular client's organizational culture, foresee the human obstacles that are not visible in the data, and strategically communicate your ideas so that they are implemented.

Phronesis helps you understand what you *can* do according to the letter of the law or the terms of a contract, and what you *should* do according to the spirit of ethical conduct.

You must learn how to become attuned to the subtleties of a situation and know how to act. Ask yourself tough questions like: "Is this action aligned with *both* my values *and* the client's interests?"

There will be times when you will be pushed into uncomfortable corners: corporate environments are fertile grounds for ethical quagmires.

Revenue pressures, stringent timelines, and complex projects can blur the lines between right and wrong. At those junctions, you will have to remind yourself that your job is not just to deliver, but it's to deliver ethically. Think of it as a two-step verification process for every decision: is it practical, and is it right?

This dilemma is nothing new. The battle between power and principle is as old as civilization itself. Take, for example, the story of *Antigone*, a tragedy Sophocles wrote over two thousand years ago.

Antigone, the play's protagonist, faces an impossible choice. Her brother Polynices has been declared a traitor, and the king, Creon, has decreed that his body must rot unburied, left to be devoured by dogs and vultures. To defy this order means death. To Antigone, some rules outweigh the authority of any ruler. She believes the divine laws, moral, eternal, and unwritten, are higher than the whims of a king. She defies Creon's edict, choosing to bury her brother and honor what she knows to be right. When confronted and threatened with death, she does not waver. "I was not born to share hatred, but to love," she says. And even more defiantly: "I will suffer nothing as great as death without glory."

Antigone's courage is not born from arrogance but from a deep commitment to principle: she shows that standing firm for what is right may cost you everything, but some prices are worth paying. In the corporate world, your refusal to cross ethical lines can be a similarly powerful act. It signals to your peers and superiors that you are committed to a standard that goes beyond quarterly revenues and client appeasement.

It says you are willing to lose battles if it means winning the war of integrity.

Now, let me add a dose of realism here: this is easier said than done! It may sound noble, but it is not always practical or desirable.

Not every junior consultant can storm into the Senior Partner's office and shout, "We shall henceforth be ethical!" without ending up on a swift exit interview. Your brave refusal might land you in career Siberia, so pick your battles wisely. A single act of refusal might send a strong message, but it's unlikely to be a tipping point unless it's part of a broader, ongoing effort to change behavior and attitudes.

Plus, refusal without constructive dialogue is just obstruction.

If you are going to say *no*, be prepared to articulate *why* and offer an alternative solution. This approach transforms your refusal into an educational moment, not a tantrum.

Let's not ignore the elephant in the room: there have been some headline-grabbing cases in recent years where big-name consultancies have crossed the line. Whether it's being involved in the opioid crisis, contributing to environmental degradation, or assisting governments in ways that led to social injustices, these instances reveal what can happen when financial gains eclipse ethical considerations.

These are institutional failures, but remember, institutions are made of people.

These stories underline that your individual ethical decisions are not simply about you; they contribute to the overall culture and reputation of your firm and the consulting industry at large. Your *Consultant's Dharma*, therefore, becomes a vital link in a chain of integrity (or lack thereof) that can either elevate or tarnish the public perception and the internal ethics of your profession.

For every parasite, many honorable people will lend you a hand

After deconstructing these complexities, I trust it's clear that living your Consultant's Dharma is about understanding that ethics is not just good policy but good business.

Many years ago, I had to deal with a colleague, let's call him Jackie, who was a pathological liar. No lie was too big or small for him, and he would not stop at anything as long as it served his purpose. He was incompetent at his job (sales) and an all-around difficult person to work with. Jackie was an odd figure for a salesman. He dressed poorly: ill-fitting shirts that always seemed slightly wrinkled, scuffed shoes that spoke of years of neglect. His entire presence reeked of decay, not in the physical sense, but in the spiritual one. He was completely unassuming, a man who could vanish into the background of any room despite working in a profession built on persuasion and charisma. His demeanor was off. His voice lacked firmness, like someone speaking in borrowed words. His handshake was limp, his posture unsure.

If he tried to sell you something, you probably would not buy it, not because of the words he used but because you could instinctively sense that there was nothing solid behind them. His existence was a counterfeit. I often wondered about his past: his desperation to manipulate, to twist reality to his advantage, felt like it came from somewhere more profound than mere ambition. It was survival, a constant state of hustling that made him prefer shortcuts over craftsmanship. He may have been overlooked too many times, and that may be why lying had become his default. In his mind, truth was not a reliable currency, so he dealt in deceit. The thing about liars and frauds is that their success depends on others buying into their illusions, but illusions break under stress, under the test of time. Truth, on the other hand, has durability; it can take punches and remain standing.

Jackie did not struggle with competence. He actively resisted it. Improvement requires acknowledging inadequacy, something he was unwilling to do. He wanted only easy wins, anything that would keep the game going a little longer. His existence was about kicking the can down the road, delaying reality from catching up (and then he kept complaining why a *senior person* like him was always ignored when promotion time came.)

I never did much business with him, but our paths crossed occasionally. Once, he asked for advice on a client pitch. I gave him a few suggestions, practical ones. He brushed them off with a snarky comment, "I think I know how to handle this." He lost the deal. I did not say anything: he was already doing the talking for both of us.

I could have taken his comment personally. I could have allowed his arrogance to provoke me and drag me down to his level, but that's the trick, right? When you respond to poison with poison, you enter someone else's game and, when you fight on their terms, you always lose.

The world is filled with people like Jackie, operators trying to win in the short term, unwilling to accept that the real game is played over decades. They live off borrowed trust, borrowed status, borrowed words. And, eventually, the credit runs out.

Instead of sinking to his level, I chose to continue doing the best work I could. I chose to keep sharpening my craft.

You cannot fix someone else's scarcity mindset or repair their brittle ego. That's not your job.

Over the long run, never compromise the boundaries you have drawn for yourself: for every parasite, many honorable people are willing to lend a hand.

Preserve your career, your team's spirit and sanity by refusing to step outside those ethical lines, no matter the temptation or provocation.

It's deceptively simple. And immensely difficult.

***

Vignette

Morrie and Ivy are sitting next to each other. Morrie is scrolling on his phone, reading an article by the Financial Times, Ivy is lost in deep thought.

Ivy: Do you know that anti-drug campaign slogan, JUST SAY NO?
Morrie [putting his phone away]: Yeah, those never worked. What about them?
Ivy: That's what I was thinking. Corporate malpractice seminars usually go, 'Say NO and Report.' But like seriously? Especially as a junior, what if it gets me fired or sidelined?
Morrie: It's like walking a tightrope over a pit full of alligators.
Ivy: While wearing a meat suit... One day, it is altering the numbers slightly, just prettying them up a teeny bit, and the next day, there is an energy crisis 'cause the projections compounded, and my back is against the wall 'cause a Russian oligarch lost money.
Morrie: Okay, Ivy. You are not Tom Cruise. We do influential work with extreme effects, but that's a little too Hollywood.
Ivy: I can write a whole series about a rogue consultant. But what should I do? "No" does not work. A "yes" is not me. And a "maybe" is just worse?
Morrie: Refusal without a plan is just obstruction. Say "NO," but be ready to explain *why*, and ask for time with other team members. Have your ethical boundaries, and stand firm. Being a good leader is more about character than competence.
Ivy: What are your ethical boundaries?
Morrie: What makes you think I have not been rogue the whole time?

***

Practical exercises

To practice the key ideas discussed in this chapter, work on the following three actionable exercises:

Ethical decision-making scenario analysis

Activity: Analyze a real-world scenario of your choice (past or present) where ethical boundaries were tested. Identify key moral issues, and reflect on your values and principles discussed in the chapter. Write down your proposed action and justification. Discuss your solution with a peer or mentor.

Objective: To develop the ability to recognize ethical dilemmas and practice making decisions that align with your moral principles and professional standards.

Crafting your ethical framework

Activity: Create your "Consultant's Dharma" by reflecting on your core values and ethical behavior. Identify potential ethical challenges in your work and define your non-negotiables. Develop strategies to address said dilemmas and push back against unethical requests. Jot down and periodically review your ethical framework.

Objective: To establish a clear set of ethical guidelines to help you navigate complex situations and maintain your integrity in the consulting profession.

***Phronesis* in practice**

Activity: Choose a recent project or define a hypothetical scenario. Identify the needed technical and practical knowledge. Consider ethical con-

siderations and their intersections. Develop a balanced plan that is effective and ethical. Discuss with a mentor or peer for insights and refinement.
Objective: To enhance your ability to apply practical wisdom in balancing technical solutions with ethical considerations, ensuring that your actions are both practical and right.

What the Hell Is It All For?

If you are a consultant, banker, lawyer, or any kind of well-paid corporate nomad, your career is an exercise in cultivated selfishness. You did not get into this line of work to *serve others* or *make the world a better place*. No, you got in because, at some point, something about the grind, the prestige, the intellectual games, and the paychecks seduced you. Admit it.

But, unlike, say, a mathematician locked in a room with his equations or a novelist who can afford to be a functional misanthrope, you do not operate in a vacuum. You exist in the real world, where people (usually those closest to you) must put up with the mess you create. The biggest casualty in this war of ambition is often the person you end up with: the spouse, the partner, the one who picks up the pieces when you return from yet another week of corporate trench warfare.

You can pretend this does not matter.

You can tell yourself that your work, your career, and your carefully optimized trajectory are all that count. But if you do not get this part of life right or solve for this asymmetry, you will wake up one day in a hotel suite, staring at the ceiling, wondering what on earth has happened to you.

This is the story of how I met the only partner that genuinely mattered (like all great stories, it started with alcohol, questionable life choices, and a series of improbable events that in retrospect look inevitable).

London used to have many absurd institutions (still has, you know what I'm referring to), but none quite as ridiculous as The Church. Of course, it was not a real church, in the sense that there were no priests or sermons or solemnity. Instead, it was a degenerate Sunday morning tradition: a nightclub that operated from 9 am to 1 pm, where people, many still wearing last night's party clothes, showed up to drink and dance, and behave like overgrown toddlers on a sugar rush. When you are 24, this kind of thing feels like a good life choice.

This was England in its purest form, where binge drinking is a sport, bad decisions are a rite of passage, and if you squint hard enough, debauchery starts to resemble culture. One Sunday, I was there for a friend's birthday, wading through the crowd with a beer in hand, when I saw her.

The Odalisque.

Blonde, blue-eyed, dressed like a courtesan from some forgotten empire. I am Italian, we appreciate aesthetics the way the English appreciate orderly queues and warm beer. This girl had style. She could also dance, which, if you have ever witnessed the rhythmic horrors of British clubbing (in my twenties I was a regular at the *On Anon* in Piccadilly Circus, hence I am an expert), you would understand is a rare and valuable trait.

In these moments, you have a choice.

The Hollywood version of events tells you to make a move immediately. Lock eyes, say something clever, sweep her off her feet. Reality is different. Reality is full of hesitation and missed opportunities. I saw her, nodded, smiled, and did precisely nothing. But fate, in its perverse wisdom, was not done with me yet.

Hours later, as the music died and people shuffled toward the coat check, I found myself standing in line. Who was behind me? The Odalisque herself.

This was the moment: one of those pure asymmetric bets that I like. Worst case, I make a fool of myself, who cares? Best case, this changes my life (remember Chapter #1). I turned around and unleashed my full Italian charm: accent, la dolce vita, the food, the culture, the whole arsenal. It worked. Technically, her friend intervened, nudging her to exchange numbers with me, but I will take the assist. I grabbed her phone, dialed my number, let it ring once, and saved her contact.

Kristie.

At this point, I had no idea I had just set off one of the most suspenseful sequences of my life. If this were a well-written novel, we would have reached the moment where the story would flow smoothly. Boy meets girl, boy texts girl, girl responds, they go on a date, and so on. But life is not a novel: it is a poorly edited mess with twists so absurd they would make a scriptwriter roll their eyes.

The following day, I did what any rational man with a working prefrontal cortex would do: I texted her.

The message bounced back.

Weird. I double-checked the number, and there was no mistake. Tried again. Bounced.

Now, I am Italian, not a Brit, so I do not just fold at the first sign of rejection. Brits are practically trained from birth to accept defeat with a polite shrug. You order a steak in London and it arrives overcooked? "Ah, well." Your flat has mold so thick it looks like abstract art? "Could be worse." Someone stomps on your foot in the Tube? *You* apologize. (hey, I hope I am not going too hard on the Brits).

Me? I was raised with a different playbook. When something fails, you try again. And if it keeps failing, you assume it's a temporary setback, most likely caused by incompetence, bad luck, or the gods having a laugh at your expense. So you try again. And again. And again, until the universe either gives in or collapses from exhaustion. When they say *no*, they mean *yes*: this was the motto.

So, I tried again.

And again.

And again.

Each time, the message bounced. At this point, a saner person would have conceded defeat, accepted that she gave him a fake number, and moved on with his life. But I have always been suspicious of the straight-forward narrative. The obvious explanation is usually too obvious. So I devised a plan. I would send one text a day, just one. A simple experiment. If, by some miracle, the network *repaired* itself, my message would finally go through.

For six days, nothing happened. My texts disappeared into the void. Then, on the seventh day (yes, the biblical overtones!) I was at the O2 Arena with friends, about to watch Roger Federer play in the ATP Finals. In the middle of the match, I suddenly remembered. I pulled out my phone, sent the message... and this time, it went through. The text had *sent*. I stared at my phone, heart pounding. This was a high stakes moment, a Schrödinger's text situation: until she replied, she both remembered me and had completely forgotten I existed.

I waited. And waited. Nothing.

Hours passed. The goat of tennis was playing at the O2, but I have no recollection of the match. My friends, useless bastards, were yelling about beautiful one-handed backhands while I was living through my own psychological thriller. Did I misread everything? Had she already moved on?

Then... ping.

She responded.

At that moment, I realized two things: 1) I was going to take this woman out for pizza; 2) If I ever met the CEO of Vodafone, I was going to punch him in the face.

We set up a date at *Rosso Pomodoro* in Notting Hill.

If you have spent even five minutes with an Italian, you know that food is not just food but a test of character. This was the moment. If she dared insult Neapolitan pizza by suggesting it needed extra toppings or, God forbid, ketchup, I would have had to reevaluate everything. Luckily, she got it. Took one bite and declared it the best pizza she had ever had.

That was it. The deal was sealed.

From that moment on, things moved fast. We clicked immediately. No social acrobatics or tedious small talk, no games, but simply two people who genuinely enjoyed being around each other.

Then came the first big test.

A few months into our relationship, my firm did what consulting firms do best: trying to ruin everything. "We need you in Hong Kong. Pack your bags." This was a career-defining opportunity, and I was not going to say no. But it also meant telling Kristie: "Hey, I know we just started dating, but what if you completely upend your life and move to another continent with me?" She had every reason to refuse. Her visa was expiring, and she had plans, actual, well-thought-out, responsible adult plans, to travel Europe before heading home to Australia. I was asking her to abandon all that for something completely uncertain. I felt pathetic. Asking someone to change their life for your career feels, in the moment, like an act of supreme selfishness, and yet, at the same time, I knew there was something real here, something worth taking a chance on.

To our credit, we handled it like grown-ups. We talked a lot about what the move meant for me, what she could do there, and what it meant for us. Ultimately, she made the insane, irrational, and absolutely correct decision. One month later, she took a plane and moved in with me. We lived at the *Grand Hyatt* in Hong Kong for a year, fully expensed. *Moët & Chandon* glasses appeared out of nowhere. The concierge greeted us like royalty. We had, for all intents and purposes, hacked life. To this day, Kristie jokes that I tricked her into marriage by making her think this was our everyday lifestyle. She was actively throwing herself into my world: while I was grinding away at work, she signed up for Italian classes. In Hong Kong.

Eventually, she slid back into finance and took a job at a local insurance firm. We built a life there, and when we finally moved back to London, it became clear that this was not just some temporary adventure. This was it.

Here is what most people never realize about careers like mine: behind every so-called *successful* consultant is an unseen partner making it possible. Kristie did not just support my career. She enabled it.

The long nights. The missed family gatherings. The constant upheaval. She handled all of it, not because she had to, but because she believed in us. I will tell you what I have learned: you do not deserve a partner like that. You earn one. Relationships, the real ones, are not built on convenience but are high-risk, high-reward investments. She bet on me. And I will spend the rest of my life proving it was the best bet she ever made.

Having someone who supports you makes you braver. You are more likely to try new things because you are not afraid of falling: you know someone is there to catch you. This team-up changes how you see your goals. Winning is not just for you anymore: it's for both of you.

In our field, when work stress hits, it usually means 80-hour work weeks, lack of sleep, and hard deadlines. In those moments, when you are staring at the mirror, brushing your teeth with one hand and self-loathing with the other, you curse yourself for your fucked-up priorities. The voice in your head starts to question everything. And that voice is loud.

We chase careers across continents like modern-day *conquistadores*, suitcases full of slides instead of muskets. Somewhere along the way, ambition became our compass, and global mobility the badge of honor. We call it growth, or opportunity, or something else, but deep down, we are just trying to outrun the silence and the terrifying question that catches up in the quiet of hotel rooms and delayed flights:

What the hell is it all for?

I have felt that silence. I have lived those flights. And I have seen, more than once, how easy it is to let the job swallow everything else: your time, your presence, your relationships, until all that remains is a name on a document and a LinkedIn profile no one reads twice.

I am not here to pretend I have it all figured out. I am not here to glorify the grind or shame the hustle. This life, the consulting life, can give you a lot, but only if you learn to draw a line. You have to decide what *enough* looks like... for *you*.

Not for your firm, not for your parents, not for the metrics, but *for you*.

In the end, all careers are temporary. What is not temporary is how you show up for the people who bet on you when they did not have to.

That is the real legacy. Everything else, every title, every bonus, every client win, fades away.

It never got easier, but it definitely became more manageable once I realized that my wife was there to sustain my journey emotionally.

This chapter won't have exercises because there is nothing I can teach you here.

You will know when you have found the right person for you.

If I look back at my story, I still cannot believe the twists and turns of luck that took my life to where it is now, and my marriage to the happiness we are living through.

I could have given up on sending that text message at least twice a day, every day, for a week, and who knows where I would be now.

Instead, I persisted: I took that girl for pizza and married her.

Oh, do you want to know why the texts kept bouncing for that first week? Turns out, right after we left The Church, her bag was stolen. She immediately blocked her cards, her phone number, everything. It took her a week to get a new SIM card, port her old number, and finally turn her phone back on. The moment she did that, the first message she received was mine.

She was in love from that moment. I had been in love since the week before.

And this, this is what it's all for.

Not the KPIs, or the status updates, and certainly not the $7 oat latte at the airport lounge while replying to emails on a Saturday.

It is for coming home. It is for the 10pm laugh when our baby *finally* gives up and sleeps like a drunk poet. It is for Sunday mornings when our dog (the unlicensed therapist he is), bursts into the kitchen like he owns the damn place. It is for dinners with no phones and no agendas (as long as there's pizza).

It is for raising a daughter who sees love not as something you find, but something you *build*, with stubbornness and humor, and with someone who helps you do the dishes without being asked.

This life I have, I did not build it alone. And now, we are building something bigger together: a family, and a legacy.

Outro

As we reach the end of this book, let me remind you: mastery of the ideas we have explored is not some neatly predictable process or an MBA case study with a clean structure, yet the road to proficiency is often much shorter than you think.

The beauty of growth, especially in our white-collar profession, lies in the fact that consistency beats elaborate planning: you do not need to wait for years and years of grueling effort to see progress. Start today. Dedicate yourself to the exercises I laid out at the end of each chapter. Think deeply, test repeatedly, discard what does not work and double down on what does. Before your next performance review, you could be 80% there.

Rapid advancement is a form of asymmetric payoff. It shows your leadership that you are not a docile cog playing by the rulebook, but a practitioner who understands that progress comes from tinkering and relentless improvement. What propels careers forward is the act of running towards that improvement: action begets results, results beget recognition and recognition creates more opportunities.

Many *intellectuals* say that the skills we discussed in this book cannot be taught, that they are some mystical, unteachable essence you either *have* or you do not. Bullshit. The real problem is not the content but the delivery. Too many people try to teach this stuff by acting like priests on a pulpit, delivering their sacred truth to the mortals below, mistaking altitude for insights. No wonder no one listens.

I am not your professor. I am just like you, only with more gray hairs (if I had any hair left on my head at all) and a few more memories.

Perhaps those *intellectuals* are even right: not everything can be taught, OK. But *everything* can be learned, if the ego is quiet, the timing is right, and the lessons are delivered by someone who still remembers what it felt like to be lost.

So no, I am not here to preach. I am here to remind, to repeat the obvious until it becomes second nature.

Most of what matters is not hidden. It is ignored.

I will leave you with a collection of (almost) random thoughts I originally published in my newsletter, Consulting Intel, fragments of my personal consulting journey, warts and all *(loosely inspired by the work of one of my favorite writers, Steven Pressfield).*

I hope this book will serve you well, and I wish you all the best in navigating the wild and unpredictable terrain of your professional and personal life.

Scattered Thoughts over Two Decades of Consulting

You can not really learn the consulting business in school.

In the real world, the process is more like serving back-to-back apprenticeships under a rogues' gallery of masters.

It happens in the office, open spaces, and conference rooms. It happens in airports and hotels. It happens after too many coffees and too many drinks.

You move to London, Amsterdam, Milan, New York, Hong Kong, and Sydney. True story.

You network.

You befriend analysts like you, slaving away putting PowerPoints together at ungodly hours.

You buddy up with the Senior Managers, Directors, and Partners, whose names are always listed first on proposals. You put in facetime, work for peanuts, and take on grunt work nobody else wants.

You teach yourself.

You tackle projects working from 7 am to 10 pm, Monday to Sunday, for 55 days in a row, with half of your team members speaking a language you can't understand. You vow you will be leading engagements *your way* before you turn 30.

On Day One as an analyst, some fast-talking senior consultant asks if you validated the KPIs to set a success baseline.

"Validated what?"

You teach yourself.

You take a training course. Then, ten more. You get PMP certified. Then TOGAF, then something else. Maybe you go back to school and study for an MBA. Eventually, you didn't, and that was your choice.

You pour over old decks and books on strategy and frameworks. You read manuals on how to write and how to think. You learn how to speak; I mean, you know how to speak, but can you persuade and influence?

Partners and managers give you harsh feedback, tearing apart all slides you submit. You are thrown in the shit, dismissed as useless, exploited as cannon fodder.

Your bosses take your time, drain your mental stamina, and run you ragged. You let them.

You let them because you know that is the price to pay to grow.

You get forwarded an email with no context. The instructions are simple: "Can you get it done?"

You teach yourself.

And you get it done.

Your consulting buddies become your network. One gets hired somewhere else in a bigger role, pulling the whole group up. You are that one.

Your boss calls, asking you to finalize a response to an RFP for a big client. By tomorrow. "Can you make it?" Of course, you can.

You teach yourself.

Alone at your laptop, struggling to answer the fundamental consulting question: *How the fuck does this shit come together?*

Creative epiphanies and breakthroughs come slowly after banging your head for hours when that intricate set of Excel formulas finally stops giving #REF! errors. Each small step forward matters when you tally small wins into big results.

Over months, years and decades, the pieces come together into a puzzle so complex you have no idea how you managed to solve it (or, did you *actually* solve it?).

You can point to a governance framework you built for a presentation you gave 4 years earlier to a client that never bought anything.

An old Partner remembers the late-night brainstorming that gave birth to a new *as-a-Service* offering that he is still selling today.

You wake up at 3 am because the Muse just whispered in your ears how to structure the exec summary for tomorrow's pitch.

Your first mentor calls to remind you of that night at the Marriott when you came up with the slide that won $10M worth of work.

Your team members have you on speed dial because they need your guidance before today's client session.

An old boss meets you after 15 years and reveals, "You were always the most curious and committed one of the lot."

"Either you do it, or we disqualify this. Nobody else can pull it off", your boss tells you.

You have learned. And you will keep learning.

Dive straight into the action early, and you will swim ahead of 99% peering timidly from the safe shallows.

Face the fire or fizzle out.

And you, my friend, were never meant for the safe shallows.

Acknowledgements

To my family: thank you for being my compass and the reason I strive for better in all things.

To my wife, whose patience and belief in me have carried me through many moments of doubt. Your quiet strength has reminded me that success and fulfillment are about having someone who sees your potential even when you lose sight.

To my daughter, whose curiosity and happiness about the world are a daily masterclass in approaching life with wonder. Watching you grow has been a humbling reminder that questions often matter more than answers, and that joy is found in the small and spontaneous moments.

To my parents, who planted the earliest seeds of fascination within me and encouraged me to chase my ambitions beyond borders (now that I am a parent, I understand how hard that must have been). I carry your wisdom in every decision I make.

Thank you to my editor Pranjal, whose insights and thoughtful challenges pushed me to clarify my voice and polish rough ideas. Writing can be isolating, but you made it a conversation rather than a monologue (sometimes, a very long conversation!).

This is my first book-writing experiment, one built on the love and contributions of many. Be kind.

This book belongs to all of you, in countless ways. Thank you for being part of this journey.

APPENDIX

THIS BOOK IN BULLETS

Serendipity strikes those who seek it

- Serendipity can be used as an active tool for career development. The corporate world is utter chaos, but chaos is not necessarily destructive.

- Proactively seeking opportunities often puts us in the 'right places', opening doors for further growth and adventure.

- The early days of consulting usually involve working on various projects and tasks. A common question that pops into every young business hotshot's head is: "Will I ever be a specialist in anything?". The key is not to perceive such tasks as random projects but as "career door openers".

- When given a choice between two gigs, always choose the one that can make you a legend, i.e., projects with low risk but disproportionate rewards. Embrace 'calculated randomness', which means conscious calculations about risks and rewards.

- Serendipity is not luck but a way of life. Attend the networking event that has nothing to do with your field, and read about emerging innovations you don't care about. Remember, no knowledge or connection is ever a waste.
- Serendipity favors those who chase it.

Wear influence, and become the one others chase

- What if instead of 'You' going to 'Them' we focus on creating opportunities so that 'They' come to 'You'? This is the fundamental mantra of Upside-Down Networking, the art of being invited to rooms you don't have any business being in.
- The key is to offer something of value, usually a fresh perspective or unique insight, without asking for anything in return, at least in that immediate moment.
- The world of consulting is primarily about forming long-term, mutually beneficial relationships. So, don't be just another junior consultant in the eyes of your seniors: *BE AN ASSET.*
- Your reputation is your currency. Mention a valuable insight in a general conversation using existing channels. Be consistent with actionable ideas. The most important thing is to be patient.
- If your insight and perspective help the Partner make better decisions, they will try to keep you close. Remember, word travels

fast among top executives.

- Flip the script. Networking is a two-way street. Being valuable to your seniors also means that top leaders and experienced decision-makers are accessible to you.

Speak like you belong, or be treated like background noise

- Master the language of your assigned industry. If you want to join the elite club, you must know the secret handshake.
- Knowing the terminology influences other people's perception of you, and opens doors that seemed out of reach before. It can make the difference between being called a passionate guy or being called out as a phony or a try-hard.
- A quick way to master business language is 'contextual learning.' Actively associate each piece of new information with a real-life scenario. Refer to case studies and read relevant news on the topic. Stories stick. Facts fade.
- A good consultant is a practical one. The aim is not just to be theoretically knowledgeable but pragmatically wise. Usually, the gap between the two exists because of communication.
- Communication is an instrument of persuasion and connection. In the right context, body language, tone, and timing craft an experience that amplifies the impact of your language.
- Knowing what to say, when, and how to say it is essential in the fast-paced, trust-based business world. Be empathetic, add a bit

of theater, and use common sense.

Reflect on thyself, question everyone else

- Acknowledge the existence of your ego. In consulting, an inflated ego can lead to loss of growth opportunities and, ultimately, revenue, as relationships between peers and clients deteriorate.

- Experience means *almost* nothing in consulting: what counts is whether you can produce the results you are requested to deliver, no matter what.

- Our failures and the accompanying criticism need to be analyzed with emotional detachment. Remember, the criticism is aimed at your work, but that reflects your current skill level, not your worth as a human being.

- Embrace *Radical Openness*. Be self-aware. Have a peer group where sharing and receiving feedback are natural. *Clarify*, *Consider*, and then *Choose* how to act. Listen actively, learn, and engage in positive talk. Finally, celebrate each of your small wins.

- Build your *Circle of Critics*. These are the people whose opinions are laced to aid your growth and not just point out your shortcomings. They assist in filtering between criticism and bad faith behavior.

Some mentors are warnings, not blueprints

- An anti-mentor teaches us valuable lessons not by exemplifying the right behaviors but rather the wrong ones.
- In consulting, much progress is made via client relations, understanding of context, and soft skills. In some cases, understanding what not to do is more important than knowing what to do.
- Anti-mentors have the potential to teach us several ideas, including the importance of delegation, the ills of micromanagement, the need for personal boundaries, and, most essentially, empathy in leadership.
- Learning from an anti-mentor doesn't mean you actively seek out poor examples; you must adapt your behaviors based on both positive and negative examples around you.
- Anti-mentors are a cautionary tale, an objective lesson in how not to manage a team or run a project.

Only fools blindly obey rules they did not write

- Traditional KPIs and metrics, such as utilization rate and client satisfaction scores, only measure parts of your performance, especially when you are still learning the ropes.
- Conventional metrics keep you in line with the firm's objective. Nail these metrics. Respect them, but don't stop there. Supplement them with other metrics that capture your unique value.

- Consult your mentor, talk to your peers, create a client feedback loop, and shadow different roles. This will help you figure out your strengths and curate a portfolio of KPIs tailor-made for you.

- Remember to capture soft metrics and then translate them into actionable goals. Document your soft skills and unique approaches in a 'brag file,' and pitch your custom KPIs during promotion or job change.

- When you expand your vision to include these additional metrics, people start seeing you in a different light. Sometimes, the most impactful plays don't appear on the stat sheet.

Sculpt your time like a surgeon and guard it like a fortress

- As a young consultant, you must have a laser-like focus on the top 20% of your tasks that will deliver 80% of the value. The 80/20 Principle enables a minority of causes, inputs, or efforts that usually lead to a majority of the results, outputs, or rewards.

- When you intentionally prioritize what to pay attention to, your utilization rate stays high, and your stress level goes down. Find the courage to drop tasks and responsibilities that do not contribute to that key 20%. Delegate them, defer them, or downright ditch them.

- As a young consultant, your most valuable asset is not (yet) your expertise or your network; it's your time. Acknowledge the limitations of your cognitive abilities and synchronize your circadian rhythm with your to-do list.

- Keep asking yourself, 'Is it really urgent?' Most things that are urgent are not actually important. Allocate your time wisely, put out the real fires, and let the other ones smolder until you can get to them.

- Attach a dollar sign to your time, and see your perspective shift as you become ruthlessly efficient. This shift in perspective becomes a fundamental life philosophy that redefines what it means to be successful over the long term.

A global consultants knows how to play everywhere

- The global grind of a consulting career offers problem-solving abilities you can't get from textbooks or local gigs. You are collecting air miles and accumulating a different kind of currency: cultural capital.

- Cultural Arbitrage allows you to leverage your understanding of local customs and behavioral nuances to transform yourself into an irresistible consulting professional beyond your technical skills. You gain 'Situational Efficiency'.

- Extensive international work travel allows you to build a broad professional network as a young consultant. The folks you meet can open future opportunities and offer novel insights. It also never hurts to be the go-to person for insights on global markets.

- Navigating cross-cultural business situations with finesse gives you a distinct edge. You have to consider the context around hierarchy, punctuality, and, of course, the language barrier.

- Misreading specific cultural cues can leave you either frustrated or perceived as rude. When you work on a project in a new cultural setting, consider it an investment. It's a career trajectory that can make you the envy of those stuck in their cultural bubbles.

No one gets promoted for following the recipe

- Adopt the mindset of a start-up CEO. Treat your projects as start-ups. Look beyond numbers and deliverables and discover new ways to connect with clients, develop creative solutions, and lead teams to make a positive impact.
- In the start-up world, you PIVOT: if something is not going right, you change course quickly. Similarly, in consulting, you focus on the next opportunity if you hit a dead end.
- Intrapreneurship, like entrepreneurship, is a team sport. Be conscious of your colleagues' strengths and weaknesses. Your most valuable resources are other consultants, analysts, and the client's staff.
- Don't try to be like your peers. Maintaining an independent course of action can lead you to build something novel and original. Step out of your comfort zone and take calculated risks.
- In the early stages of your career, you are paradoxically in a

uniquely fortunate position to take calculated risks that those senior to you can't afford. Take advantage of this freedom and flexibility to be creative and innovative.

Use humor to make work sustainable

- In a world full of overly serious, self-important consultants, being playful, humorous, and self-aware gives you a distinct advantage early in your career. Humor is not a distraction: it is approachability, and, when done well, a Trojan horse for influence.

- The consultant with wit and well-timed irreverence can cut through hierarchy and speak uncomfortable truths without triggering defensive responses.

- A self-created, funny persona can disarm clients and colleagues, making interactions more human. Clients remember you not for perfect slide decks, but for shared moments of levity.

- Humor is only powerful when authentic: forced or needy humor backfires. Good humor in consulting is subtle, timely, and often self-deprecating: it enhances your status by showing confidence, not desperation.

- Self-deprecating humor is a double-edged sword: it builds trust and relatability (via the *pratfall effect*), but only works if you are already seen as competent. Overuse can undermine authority. The key is balance, know when to laugh at yourself and when to let silence carry weight.

- Use humor surgically, not constantly. Strategic humor, paired with moments of calm presence, sends a powerful message: you are confident, self-aware, and comfortable in your skin.

Be remembered as brilliant

- If you are a young consultant, you are sitting on a gold mine of opportunity to shape how people perceive you. No baggage, a clean slate, and rooms full of people who are ready to form an opinion about you.

- Consistently deliver quality work. Nothing tanks your reputation faster than sloppy deliverables. Anything other than quality screams carelessness. "Iterate Later" should never mean "Ignore the Errors Now."

- Focus on knowing your audience. In the consulting environment, you have Partners hell-bent on revenue, managers focused on utilization rates, and peers concerned with the delegation of grunt work. Maintain a balance and be strategic.

- Always be mindful of the context. Consider the subtle nuances of corporate culture and client expectations. You must selectively illuminate your successes in a way that casts a favorable glow on those around you.

- Use self-promotion as a tool. If you know how you naturally come across, you can calibrate your actions to shape perceptions better. So go ahead and be your PR agency.

- Align yourself with a mentor who's got clout but also matches your work ethic and style. You can only learn from associating with leaders; in the long run, they act as a catalyst in your career progression.

The wise grow what others long for

- If you are in consulting for a hefty bonus and an ego boost, your journey is going to be short-lived. There is nothing inherently evil about external motivators, but they are ultimately unsatisfying in the long run.

- Consulting is a demanding job. Therefore, enjoying work for work's sake, such that solving problems becomes the reward, is critical for a sustained, long-term career in the game.

- Finding your intrinsic motivators is not a one-off thing. It is an ongoing process of introspection and fine-tuning. With time, your WHY might vary, but the key is to keep that internal compass calibrated.

- Do some soul-searching and map your passion to your goal. When external pressures mount up, defend your intrinsic ideals. Create reminders and measure your progress. As you gain experience, revisit and reevaluate your motivators.

- Consulting is a people business. Seek first to understand the people, and the technical problems and solutions will come into focus. Emotional and soft skills appreciate with time while technical skills depreciate with time.

- Day-to-day consulting work is an opportunity to practice and get better at understanding people and our interaction with technology and businesses.

Take the shortcut that makes the road longer

- As you progress in your career, you must have individual ethical guardrails that you stick to even under pressure: Rules of engagement you refuse to breach, no matter the stakes.

- In consulting, even simple ethical gray spots can have a domino effect on your client, firm, and the industry. Navigating this ethical labyrinth requires emotional intelligence and situational awareness.

- Revenue pressures, stringent timelines, and complex projects can blur the lines between right and wrong. Your job is not just to deliver; it is to deliver ethically. Think of it as a two-step verification process for every decision: is it practical and right?

- Refusal without constructive dialogue is just obstruction. Say "NO", but be prepared to articulate why and offer an alternative solution. Transforming your refusal into an educational moment genuinely contributes to an ethical culture.

- Headline-grabbing cases involving big-name consultancies are institutional failures, but remember, institutions are made of people. Your individual ethical decisions are not just about you; they contribute to your firm's overall culture and reputation and the consulting industry at large.

Printed in Dunstable, United Kingdom

64611548R00151